THE CREATIVE GUIDE TO
DRIED FLOWERS

THE CREATIVE GUIDE TO
DRIED FLOWERS

CAROL PETELIN

with photographs by
Simon McBride

Webb & Bower

MICHAEL JOSEPH

To Jessica and Jason

First published in Great Britain 1988 by
Webb & Bower (Publishers) Limited
5 Cathedral Close, Exeter, Devon EX1 1EZ
in association with Michael Joseph Limited
27 Wright's Lane, London W8 5TZ

Published in association with the Penguin Group
Penguin Books Ltd, Registered Offices: Hardmonsworth, Middlesex, England
Viking Penguin Inc, 375 Hudson Street, New York, NY 10014, USA
Penguin Books Australia Ltd, Ringwood, Victoria, Australia
Penguin Books Canada Ltd, 2801 John Street, Markham, Ontario, Canada L3R 1B4
Penguin Books (NZ) Ltd, 182–189 Wairau Road, Auckland 10, New Zealand

Designed by Vic Giolitto

Production by Nick Facer/Rob Kendrew

First impression 1988
Second impression 1990
Third impression 1990

Text Copyright © 1988 Carol Petelin
Photographs Copyright © 1988 Simon McBride

Line drawings by Andrew Condrom

British Library Cataloguing in Publication Data

Petelin, Carol
  The creative guide to dried flowers.
  1. Dried flower arrangement
  I. Title
  745.92   SB449.3.D7
  ISBN 0-86350-193-1 (hardback)

Typeset in Great Britain by P&M Typesetting Ltd, Exeter, Devon

Colour reproduction by Mandarin Offset, Hong Kong

Printed and bound in Hong Kong

CONTENTS

INTRODUCTION

Fresh flowers bloom and then vanish without a trace, their beauty only a fleeting moment to savour in your home. Dried flowers, however, will last for years. The art of drying flowers has been with us for centuries, but has recently enjoyed a popular revival. Not too long ago it was not possible to buy a wide variety of dried flowers and grasses – the small choice that was available was usually to be found on local stalls in village fêtes or in one's own garden. Now dozens of shops have started selling these beautiful keepsakes and commercial growing has developed into a thriving industry.

As a child, I started collecting little seed pods and bunches for drying and I think that we all, as children, used to snatch at sweet-smelling lavender bushes from people's front gardens or in parks! Many patient hours were spent making lavender bags from the dried florets but now, with a little more thought and inspiration, lavender can be woven into baskets or bunched *en masse* into an arrangement to release that distinctive fragrance into a room. This book aims to lend a guiding hand to those who wish to create their own dried flower displays without becoming too bogged down by technicality. It concentrates principally on design: with the emphasis on visual instruction it looks at displays for the home or business, showing you how to match flowers to the colours, fabrics and overall style of your house or office.

You don't need talent or an artist's imagination, just patience and time when selecting your flowers. If you find arranging difficult, just stuff the bunches into their container, they will still look delightful. For those of you who want to experiment on a larger scale, the many ideas shown in each section of this book provide ample scope for the creative mind.

There really are very few rules for arranging dried flowers – many will argue there are none – but some uncomplicated guidelines will, if followed, simplify your task. For instance, when you are selecting flowers from an overwhelming choice, stay with a basic colour and choose as many different shapes as you can afford – the greater the variety of shapes the better the effect. If choice is limited go for masses of one type, they will look equally stunning when bunched together. I have set out an index detailing the flowers that are available commercially, though, naturally, this list is not definitive.

Flowers show nature in her best light, obviously the longer we can keep these beautiful things the greater our pleasure. The creation of eye-catching designs or the simple use of shape and form is, like most art forms, a matter of trial and error. For the dedicated enthusiast, however, this book is an invaluable companion.

Holland grows more than
seventy-five different varieties
of flowers which are suitable
for drying.

CHAPTER 1

FLOWERS GROWN FOR DRYING

HOME GROWN FLOWERS

Wherever you live in the world, you will be able to find flowers which will be suitable material for drying. The everlasting strawflowers (*Helichrysum bracteatum*) are an old faithful and have been popular for decades. They offer an excellent range of colour: deep rusts, vivid oranges, yellows, salmon, bright pink, shell pink and cream. The soil determines the variation of shade. These flowers must be harvested as soon as the flower is starting to bloom, because they continue to come out for days after they have been picked and hung for drying. They will, if picked too late, almost turn themselves inside out and become most unattractive.

Another successful family is the achillea. There are at least five colours to choose from, all varying slightly in shape. The most common, golden yarrow or *Achillea filipendulina*, can grow to great heights and is excellent for large arrangements and economically filling gaps in displays. There is another yarrow variety called 'moonshine' (*Achillea taygetea*), these can also grow to be

Mixed border of home-grown garden flowers suitable for drying.

A glorious field of pink poker (*Limonium suworowii*) which will produce hundreds of bunches. This area in Holland is completely sand based and the flowers thrive on it.

quite large with a distinctive halo of creamy lemon. My favourite is the 'pearl'. This magnificent achillea has the most fabulous creamy white bobbles which look almost frothy in texture. The pearl air-dries beautifully and is a wonderful substitute for gypsophila. There is also a slightly smaller yarrow, flat-headed like the filipendulina but smaller and comes in a variety of pinks and mauves. *Alchemilla mollis*, commonly called lady's mantle, is a delight when dried – a soft, yellowy green haze of little florets. Pick this flower in bloom and hang it to dry in a well-ventilated, warm room, making sure that the stems are separated from each other so as not to stifle or squash the flowers.

Another hazey plant is gypsophila, an easy plant to grow and dry. When in mid-bloom bring the stems into the house and stand them in a small amount of water until the flowers have dried out. You can add glycerine to gypsophila, but this will produce a completely different effect. The flowers will not be as white and the bobbles will appear to be very slightly sticky. This method is very good for preserving the flower and does stop the tiny bobbles from falling when over dry.

The delphinium family are spectacular and fresh, their naturally muted tones become even more accentuated when dried. Support these very tall flowers with a stave to prevent them from tumbling in an impromptu summer wind or hail storm.

When peonies bloom, their life span is so short that unless you take full advantage of this moment you could miss it altogether. For best results, pick the buds just as they are about to explode into bloom, and hang them in an airing cupboard or in a warm, well-ventilated room until completely dry.

Cornflowers are easy to grow but they are quite tricky to dry. Again, this is a flower that must be picked in bud, otherwise the flowers tend to shrink completely, or the extremely vivid blue will pale around the edges, making it look dead rather than dried. A far better blue flower to dry is love-in-a-mist or *Nigella damascena*, this is a softer blue but dries very successfully when picked in flower, and is of double value since you can also dry the stripy pods when the flowers have finished.

There are many other varieties for you to try such as bottle brush, acroclineum daisies, rhodanthe, amaranthus, commonly known as love-lies-bleeding, pink poker, golden rod, tansy, Chinese lanterns, honesty – the list is endless.

COMMERCIALLY GROWN FLOWERS

Acres and acres of flowers are now grown world-wide especially for drying. This enormous increase is due to commercial demand from all parts of the Continent. At one time, one could only obtain small amounts from local growers, usually these were the good old faithful statice or helichrysum strawflower. These are known as 'everlasting' flowers since their paper-like quality comes from the flower heads that will dry out naturally when left on the plant. In recent years the dried flower industry has progressed beyond all imagination; growers are now experimenting with any variety which is likely to dry well. Techniques are quite different: once, flowers were just hung to dry, now, in Holland for example, huge drying rooms, rather like saunas, throw out heat of approximately 60°C, with a strong airflow circulating between the bunches enabling the flowers to dry out in anything between twenty-four to forty-eight hours. This quick method means that the quality of drying and the final colour of the flowers is of a very high standard. Roses are the main beneficiary of the 'sauna' method. The only flower air-dried in Holland is the hydrangea. In Holland the area reserved for growing flowers for drying is very small, particularly as a sand-based soil is required, but the annual harvest is colossal. One company alone is producing over three million bunches a year, the vast majority for export. Most of the flowers go to Germany and Austria, where dried flowers have been popular for years. They are typically incorporated with nuts, spices and silk flowers to form magnificent garlands, bouquets and hanging spheres. France grows a large quantity of flowers, mainly for its own market, but nothing like the scale of the operation in Holland. France imports from Holland, and also from Italy, another large producing country. Italy specializes in grasses, foliage and cones, whereas Holland concentrates on quality flower growing.

Since land is in short supply in Holland, farmers buy seed from the flower companies, then sell the bunches back to the same flower companies. This simple method works extremely well, allowing the flower company gradually to increase its turnover each year without any extra capital outlay on land. Fields of an amazing array of colour are spread out over this very flat area of land; teenagers are

A field of pink and white rhodanthe daisies – the colours of strawberry and vanilla ice-cream.

Harvested flowers awaiting collection for sorting.

Gomphrena thrives in warm conditions. The colourful, clover-like flower heads make ideal winter decoration when dried.

Young people are recruited from all over the area during the harvest. Here the flowers are being sorted into bunches for drying.

A colourful lavender field in Norfolk, England. Most of the English lavender comes from here.

employed during the summer months to cut flowers and sort them into the bunches ready to hang for drying. More casual labour will be sorting after the drying to check the quality and re-bunch the flowers into the correct sizes ready for packaging. Holland grows at least seventy-five different varieties of flowers, not to mention all the different colours which are common in some types. The flowers imported from other countries, such as Africa and Australia, are quite extraordinary. These amazing flowers and 'exotica' arrive dried and are then sorted, bunched and repackaged: it is a rapidly expanding market.

England grows a small amount of flowers for drying, particularly lavender, which is mainly grown in Norfolk. As you approach these magnificent fields the most incredible sight awaits, and the aroma fills the air. The density of the colour plays strange games with the light over the hills and often creates incredible sunsets. There are many lavender varieties – very pale lilac lavender, pink and also white – in addition to the common blue points sold all over the world and grown in millions of gardens. A versatile plant, it is not only used for flower decoration but also for beauty products, lavender bags and pot-pourri.

Africa produces very large quantities of flowers, and is another country which has suddenly increased its production. Principal varieties grown include little everlasting daisies, *Helichrysum vestium*, curry plant and achillea, fabulous leaves and proteas producing plants with pretty bobbles. Their dying techniques are excellent and create the most wonderful variation of pastel apricots and pinks in all these flowers. Look out for the daisies being sold commercially, they give an attractive translucence to an arrangement.

Australia, too, has wild flowers that have suddenly become commercially viable; so much so that some are near extinction and picking is now controlled in certain areas governed by protection orders. The flowers that you will be most likely to encounter are the orange morrison, red bottle brush and very unusual kangaroo paw.

For those who do not have a garden, or lack the time to grow flowers for drying, specialist shops are at last offering an acceptable alternative. These shops usually sell all the essential materials in addition to a wide range of dried flowers. The enthusiast now has ample scope to create visually impressive, and long-lasting, floral displays.

Inset
Lavender basket

The flowers, now in bunches, are being sorted and hung in huge racks which will be transported down to the drying rooms.

Bunches of white rhodanthe daisies prior to sorting.

DRYING AND PRESERVATION TECHNIQUES

Air-drying

If you have a reasonably large garden, it is a good idea to grow all the flowers for drying in one area, rather like the vegetable patch, especially as there are unattractive gaps after harvesting. Shrubs such as hydrangeas or rose bushes can also be grown for drying. If you are buying rose bushes, choose multi-flowered rather than singular-flowered varieties, these will air-dry easily – other large, single blooms will be more fragile and have to be dried using the desiccant technique. I was recently given a bunch of red rose buds, and when they were past their best, after a couple of days, they went into my airing cupboard for a week where they dried beautifully. They now occupy a permanent place on my desk.

Hydrangeas are very rewarding flowers to dry. Their colour will vary with soil type, but unlike most flowers, you should harvest them when they are practically dried on the bush. This is very late in the season and each little

16

centre stamen on the florets has disappeared. Remove the leaves and crush the base of the stem with a mallet or a rolling pin. Stand them in about two inches of water in a warm (not hot) atmosphere and they will dry out in approximately ten days. They will feel crisp, and occasionally the odd one will fail. I personally find the deep pink variety the easiest to dry and the blue the hardest. It is often a question of trial and error.

One can experiment with almost any flower but to catch them at their best remember to harvest your flowers just as they are emerging from bud. Do not pick the flowers when it has just rained, wait until they are as dry as possible, allowing plenty of time for any morning dew to evaporate.

Annuals can be grown with relative ease, either in tandem with other flower types or in specially designated parts of the garden. Try growing as many colours and shapes as possible, thus broadening your scope for arrangements, or for hanging *en masse* on your ceiling or wall. Dried flower bunches make beautiful presents: try making little bouquets for friends at Christmas, or create your own place settings for an important dinner party.

The desiccant technique
Some flowers are not really suitable for drying. Daffodils, tulips, crocuses and irises are particularly tricky, mainly because they are rather fleshy and contain too much water, but you could experiment by drying them using a desiccant or drying agent. There are several sorts of desiccant, but by far the easiest and quickest is silica gel, obtainable from most chemists. This chemical is not cheap, but it can be used over and over again. There are two types: one has a built-in colour indicator, turning the crystals from pink when there is moisture present to blue when the crystals are moisture free; the other type of crystal is white. Both types are made up of large crystals which must be ground down. A coffee grinder or pestle and mortar are ideal for this job. Remember to clean both after use. Fill an airtight container with the silica gel, first making sure the container is bone dry. Place the desiccant in a low oven for an hour. Turn the oven off and allow it to cool thus ensuring that no moisture remains. All sorts of flowers can be dried in this way; it is advisable to wire the stems before placing them in the gel as they do tend to be more fragile afterwards. Silica gel requires no heat while drying, unlike other methods.

The process should take between one and five days, depending on the plant type. The plant material must be completely covered with the powder, but before you spoon on the powder, take a paint brush and gently coat the inside petals with the silica gel so that no area escapes. All materials going into the desiccant must be perfect, any flaws will be accentuated and look ugly.

When you remove the dried plant material, make sure none of the powder is clinging to the petals. Again using a dry, clean paint brush gently brush the powder off the petals back into the container.

All the following flowers are suitable for desiccant preservation: roses, peonies, camellias, carnations, clematis, Christmas roses, marigolds, lilac, mimosa, orchids, pansies, passion flowers, primroses and zinnias.

The glycerine technique
Apart from flowers, all sorts of leaves can be preserved using glycerine: eucalyptus, beech, oak, pittosporum, ivy, bay, horse chestnut, to name but a few. One should pick the leaves at their absolute best. I often pick beech leaves right through the summer, at different intervals, thus obtaining different variations of colour when they have been glycerined. The leaves always go darker and less green than when fresh, but give a beautiful rich glow to displays.

Everyone has a favourite method when glycerining, I have found the following to be very successful: firstly, choose a sturdy container, preferably a metal bucket, a plastic one will do, making sure that the sides are high enough to prevent the branches from making the container top heavy and easy to overbalance. Sort through the leaves you have picked and only use the ones that are in very good condition – any leaves which are badly torn or have crackled round the edge should be discarded, or the individual leaf snipped off. Mix one tablespoon of salt to one gallon of hot water and immerse the branches in this mixture for twenty-four hours. It is advisable to crush or split the ends of the branches to ensure maximum penetration of the liquid to the tip of the leaves. When this initial process is complete, again mix hot water with the glycerine, this time in a separate container, the hotter the water, the better the glycerine will mix. Remember, the glycerine is heavy and will sink to the bottom if not mixed well. Now stand the branches in the bucket. Naturally if

An old wicker laundry basket is extremely useful for storing dried flowers. The gaps in the basket weave are perfect for letting in sufficient air to prevent the flowers from sweating and subsequently rotting.

there is a large amount of leaves you will have to double or treble the quantities of the mixture, which should be approximately one part glycerine to two parts water. The process will take about a week to complete; you will notice that the leaves will become quite sticky and little beads of glycerine will gather on the branches. These can be wiped off with a warm damp sponge. Check the level of the mixture during this time as larger branches will absorb more than a strip of ivy. The mixture can be reused but should always be heated to ensure the best result. If you are only treating a few branches, make the mixture up in a small jar; stand the smaller container in the bucket so that the leaves still have something to support their weight.

The leaves will turn various shades of dark green, or even brown if picked quite late in the season. Try adding green dye to the water if you want them to have a brighter hue. Use a

soluble dye that can be absorbed by the plants during the glycerining process. If you want to drain the colour from the plant, bleach should be added to the water (about one tablespoon to one gallon of water), you could then add a pretty pastel colour to a fresh gallon of water, to change completely the appearance of the leaves. These leaves, when preserved, should have a relatively long life. The green leaves make excellent Christmas decorations, and the lightly coloured ones might enhance a bare corner, creating beautiful shadows. Do not place these leaves beside great heat, they will shrivel.

If you do not have trees in your garden, perhaps a neighbour will let you have some branches, alternatively, a walk in the countryside will offer a wide choice, but pick sparingly, never denude one part of a tree, take a little from several trees if possible. Hedgerows and fields will produce all sorts of

18

different plant life that does not grow in gardens. Pick unusual flowers and if they are not suitable for air-drying, maybe you could try pressing them between sheets of blotting paper. Choose some eye-catching seed heads to make your dried flower arrangement into an original and interesting shape.

STORAGE

The correct storage of flowers is very important and there are some very precise methods of storing dried flowers. You may have a surplus of harvested flowers to store, or you may change your arrangements each season. Whatever the reason, a box or large basket with a lid is the best container. The box must have holes, if it does not punch some yourself, using a sharp knife or a pointed tool. You will need a quantity of tissue paper and perhaps some paper packing. Never store flowers in plastic bags or containers, they will sweat and rot in a very short time; they must have access to air, and they should be stored in the dark. Each bunch should be wrapped individually and, in the case of larger flowers, each stem should be wrapped separately in order to obtain the best results.

Place the heaviest bunches at the bottom of the container and the lighter more fragile ones at the top where they will not get squashed. Do not overload the container, it is more advisable to pack two or three if you have large quantities of flowers. Florists often have long delivery boxes that they are pleased to off-load, and shoe boxes are ideal as they often come complete with tissue paper.

These are some useful tips for looking after your dried flowers:

1 To prevent the flowers from quickly fading, do not place them in direct sunlight.
2 To prevent the flowers from dropping once arranged, lightly spray them with hair lacquer from about eighteen inches.
3 Keep them out of the reach of little children, pets and general family traffic.
4 To clean them, dust lightly with a feather duster or use a hair-dryer on a very low speed.
5 Cats love eating gypsophila!
6 Leaves can be wiped gently with a warm damp sponge, but they must be dried with a soft cloth afterwards.
7 Dried flowers hate water and damp. Ensure that they are not placed next to a damp wall or hung in a very damp room, they will develop mildew quite quickly.
8 Dried flowers love warm houses; they are ideally suited to central heating whereas fresh flowers will quickly die.
9 Dried flowers store well for years.

If you take note of the points above, your dried flowers could last for up to five years.

CHAPTER 2
SHAPES AND TYPES

Fresh flowers offer the most enormous variety of shape and colour, some of the flower heads being very large indeed. These same flowers reduce in size dramatically when dried – the only really large flower head is the hydrangea. Therefore, when you wish to create a display, particularly a large one, the more shapes and sizes you include, the greater your chances of success. This rule also applies to the smallest arrangement – the choice of at least three flower types will make all the difference.

Listed in chart form below the information on each shape type, are some interesting combinations. They run in colour order, and are a suggestion, not a hard and fast rule. There should be something for everyone.

FOLIAGE

Leaves mix well with any colours and most flower types, but really come into their own when combined with arrangements where oranges, yellows, creams and natural woody colours predominate. If the leaves have been glycerined (see Chapter 1) they will take on an even darker hue and usually a lovely warm shine. The extra height is ideal for any large arrangement, especially for the fireplace and large floor displays, and leaves are ideal for making Christmas arrangements, such as swags and garlands, (see Chapters 5 and 8). Eucalyptus leaves are treated in many different ways, from applying glycerine mixed with dye to the green leaves to bleaching and re-dying in subtle pastel colours. They are beautiful in any form, although often costly to buy, so you are indeed lucky if you have a tree in your garden.

Combinations

Beech leaves/oak/pittosporum
rust or orange helichrysum
Chinese lanterns
morrison
carthamus
matecaria
green hydrangea

Eucalyptus leaves
pink roses, white acroclinium
gypsophila

Oak leaves
yellow roses
curly grass
cones or wooden-type exotica
alchemilla
flax

SEED HEADS

Allium, poppy heads, nigella, scabious, honesty, graspin, corn-on-the-cob, Chinese lanterns, clematis, physocarpus

Seed heads and pods must be used very carefully, for if they are used in combination with very fragile or delicate flowers, the display will look clumsy. The stems are usually thicker and if visible will create an unbalanced effect. Seed heads are most impressive when used on their own, perhaps with leaves and grasses, or in large arrangements where a large quantity of flower-types has already been used.

Combinations

Poppy
pink rhodanthe
pink helichrysum
lilac statice
gypsophila

Nigella pods
pink and white larkspur
red amaranthus
pink poker
white rhodanthe

Allium (leek head)
achillea
blue hydrangea
pink rhodanthe
gypsophila

GRASSES AND WISPY FERN-TYPE PLANTS

Oats, wheat, barley, phalaris, African grass, polypogon, canary grass, briza or quaking grass

Green ferns, ambrociana, sea lavender caspia, sea lavender

Grasses and ferns are wonderful fillers and usually very economical, and being mostly green, they blend beautifully with any assortment. Placed singularly or in small clumps wired together, they are equally effective, giving some movement and softness to the general appearance of the display. The sea lavenders are the classic base for any basket or vase, making gaps and mistakes vanish in

Opposite
A selection of pittosporum, dyed pink and apricot eucalyptus leaves, bleached eucalyptus leaves, beech leaves, oak leaves, ruscus and Australian holly oak.

seconds! Being generally white or white/grey in colour they are suitable for any colour combination you wish to try.

Combinations

Oats
red roses

Ambrociana
green amaranthus
pink roses
gypsophila

Phalaris
lilac larkspur
lilac statice
achillea pearl
matecaria
sea lavender

Adianthum
pink statice
pink phalaris
pink rhodanthe
white *Helichrysum vestium*
baby star
caspia

A mixture of adiantum, ambrociana, quaking grass, sea lavender, oats, phleum, *Limonium caspia*, phalaris, festuca, pampas grass and *Bromus formus*.

Opposite
Scabious heads, bells of Ireland, teasles, nigella pods, flax, Chinese lanterns, honesty and poppy heads – a chunky, colourful display.

This basket is filled with yellow
African everlasting daisies,
white *Helichrysum vestium*,
pink acroclinium daisies, pink
baby star, pink and white
rhodanthe daisies, various
shades of pink helichrysum,
yellow helichrysum and lilac
and white xeranthemum.

24

DAISY-TYPE FLOWERS

Rhodanthe daisies in pink and white, acroclinium daisies in pink or white, subulifolium daisy, ammobium daisy, silene, xeranthemum, *Helichrysum vestium*, African everlasting daisy, helichrysum strawflowers

These incredibly versatile flowers, perhaps slightly more common and available than some dried flowers, are wonderful in so many arrangements. Rhodanthe daisies, which come in either pink or white, are particularly adaptable.

With small arrangements, cut the flowers down to the length you require, do not let the length of the stems hamper your style; for a larger effect try wiring a quarter of the bunch together to make a larger splash of colour. At this point great care is required as some daisy heads tend to fall off easily, a tube of glue or a glue gun are useful tools to have close to hand. Daisies will go with any arrangement and have a softening effect on what can sometimes be too stark a display; beware not to leave them exposed to very bright sunlight as they will fade quite quickly.

Combinations

Pink rhodanthe
nigella
amaranthus red
pink helichrysum
caspia

Lilac and white xeranthemum
poppy heads
lilac larkspur
lilac statice
cream broom bloom

White acroclinium
yellow helichrysum
lonas
achillea pearl
ambrociana/lipidium

LARGE, FLAT-HEADED FLOWERS

Achillea, dahlia, hydrangea, *Verticordia brownii* 'morrison', peony, helichrysum, celosia

These large flower types, which are ideal for filling obvious gaps, are in very short supply.

The only way to get round this problem is to wire a mass of heads of one type of flower together to form a large false head and create a splash of colour. Hydrangeas used on their own are extremely attractive and will last for years. They will fade however, but their naturally muted colours seem to become even more attractive with time. There is a lovely china-blue species of hydrangea, which is the most difficult to dry, but if successful, the resulting shade of blue justifies the effort.

Combinations

Yellow achillea
white rhodanthe
pink larkspur
blue nigella bloom
alchemilla

Pink hydrangea
red roses
gypsophila
sea lavender

Blue hydrangea
alchemilla
lavender
gypsophila
pink statice

Morrison
carthamus
oats/ambrociana
beech leaves

ROUND SHAPES AND THISTLE TYPES

Sea holly, echinops, carthamus, teasles, sterlingia, centoria, globe artichoke

This particular shape is very useful but often extremely prickly to use. There are dozens of varieties of sea holly, a number of them grow wild on hills in Europe. It would seem that the hotter the climate, the darker grey they become; the Northern European varieties are an extremely pleasing blue, which has an extraordinary irridescence when placed in certain light. The most common variety sold commercially is typified by small-headed bobbly clusters, while the larger variety has a large head and is noted for its vivid shade of blue. Some other thistle types are more orangey, but equally prickly! Centoria is a

A medley of helichrysum,
peonies, hydrangea, achillea,
cockscomb, leek heads,
Australian *Verticordia brownii*
and morrison.

majestic large-headed, tall thistle; being a curious shade of yellow it is marvellous for very large arrangements.

Combinations

Sea holly
monkshood
lavender
matecaria
pink peonies
red amaranthus
pink rhodanthe

Teasles
beech leaves
white rhodanthe
yellow achillea
salmon helichrysum
caspia

Sea holly/echinops
achillea pearl
white *Helichrysum vestium*
oats/ambrociana
pink peonies

Various sea holly, hops, sterlingia, centaurea, *Carthamus ionas*, gomphrena and matecaria.

27

SPIKY FLOWERS

Larkspur, amaranthus, statice, *Limonium suworowii* (pink poker), solidago, golden rod, lavender, monkshood, caspia, ti-tree

These flowers often form the shape for large vases. The triangular form, especially in flat-backed displays, is useful for breaking up a flat look or cushion effect – frequently a problem when using larger flowers. It is generally a good rule to have at least one spiky flower in an arrangement.

Larkspurs are varied in colour and height, delphiniums, their bigger counterpart, are even taller with larger blooms, and are excellent when positioned at the back of the display to gain height. The colours are usually pinks, mauves and whites, but are more muted when dried. Monkshood is similar in appearance though a deeper, truer blue than the blue varieties of the delphinium family – although many people are unable to differentiate between them when they are dried. They are also very poisonous so should not be placed within reach of children or household pets.

Combinations

Caspia
pale pink helichrysum
poppy heads
caspia
pink rhodanthe

White larkspur
dill
cream helichrysum
white acroclinium daisy
phalaris

Pink larkspur
pink rhodanthe
red roses
gypsophila
sea lavender

TINY-HEADED AND CLUSTER-TYPE FLOWERS

Gypsophila, anaphalis, glixia, alchemilla, dill, statices, silene, sanfordii, solidaster, curry plant, broom bloom, seacrest, limoniums

Most of these flowers are ideal for softening the overall effect of an arrangement.

Alternatively, they can be extremely effective when used on their own. A cloud of gypsophila or alchemilla looks enchanting, particularly to enhance a bedroom or to soften a corner with a wall bouquet. Little clusters of glixia or solidaster can be used to form the large-headed flowers described above; any of these wonderful bunches look particularly effective hanging from rafters in a kitchen or living-room. Rustic houses seem to show dried flowers off to their maximum splendour. If you are fortunate enough to have an old-beamed ceiling in your kitchen, gypsophila and alchemilla are two types that are simple to dry from your garden or from a bunch purchased in a market place.

Combinations

Pink glixia
pink baby star or *Helichrysum vestium*
oats
achillea pearl

Alchemilla
white larkspur
pink roses
achillea pearl
green hydrangea
caspia

Dill
nigella bloom
matecaria
pale pink peonies
pale pink hydrangea
oats

Gypsophila
Use on its own, in abundance

ROSE TYPES

Roses, peonies, dahlias, chrysanthemums

Roses dry so beautifully and the varieties one can now obtain commercially have increased considerably. There are at least three shades of red, five sorts of pink and mauve, some stripy types and two sorts of yellow, one quite bright and the other nearer apricot. They will dry well straight from your garden if picked when quite dry and placed in a warm airing cupboard or hung from your kitchen rafters. Peonies, once dried, are frequently confused with roses, and are often even more spectacular. The colours

Opposite
Sea lavender, statice, golden rod, lavender, basilia, pink poker, love-lies-bleeding, lipidium, ti-tree, kangaroo paw, larkspur and caspia.

29

Statices, curry flower, solidaster, alchemilla, broom blooms, silene, gypsophila, achillea 'pearl'.

Opposite
Yellow, cream, pink and red roses and assorted pink and cream peonies make up the glorious colours in this glass vase.

are not quite so varied, but they are one of the most useful large, soft-coloured flower heads to have in your repertoire. If you do not possess a peony plant, perhaps a willing neighbour could let you have a couple of heads when they first start to flower. All these types can be gently unfurled to look even larger, but try steaming them for a few minutes first, because if they are too dry they will simply disintegrate in your hands. Be warned, the prickles on roses when dried are an even greater threat, so a pair of lightweight gardening gloves is a useful accessory.

Combinations

Red roses
cream helichrysum
green ruscus
white broom bloom
sea lavender
(excellent Christmas combination)

Deep pink peonies
gypsophila
green hydrangeas

Pink roses/pink chrysanthemum or dahlias
white African everlasting daisy
alchemilla
sea lavender

30

A mixture of African and
Australian plants including
barbigera, curly grass,
Leucodendron plumosom, woody
pear, various types of protea,
jacaranda pods, silver brunia,
bell cup stems, salignum,
paranomous, recondita and
Repens supurcuts.

EXOTICA

Proteas, banksias, lotus pods, canella, platyspernum, *Leucodendron plumosum*, golden mushrooms, palm spears, bell cups, sponge mushrooms, *Dryandra formosa*

Exotica looks best when arranged on its own, but the odd piece placed in a large autumnal arrangement or Christmas display will look quite unusual. Exotica is frequently large and clumsy to deal with, so a good deal of thought is required before embarking on a display. Often a large wooden bowl on a table filled with a quantity of different varieties creates an 'arrangement' in itself. 'Trees' can be made out of sponge mushrooms: place them on sticks and line a pot with moss for a most unusual display. A single stem placed in a narrow-necked jar or vase can look impressive despite its simplicity.

Combinations

Protea
eucalyptus
curly grass
bell cup grass
yellow roses
jacaranda pods

Banksia
bell cups
Leucodendron plumosum
Dryandra formosa

Cup leaf hakea
bottle brush
curly grass
yellow *Verticordia brownii*

CONTAINERS

You probably have a container in your home which will be a perfect receptacle for flower arranging: an old pot which has been re-glued and is no longer suitable for holding water; an old kettle or teapot which has lost its lid; a jam jar – all such seemingly useless objects are suitable. I have divided this section into container type – your choice will depend on your own taste and the type of display you want to create. You may choose a container to match the flowers; alternatively, you may have a container in your home that will suit a particular room, in which case the flowers will be chosen to complement the surroundings. Natural materials suit dried flowers best of all: terracotta, basketware, wood and rough pottery are perfect, or a silver salver cascading with flowers as a table centre for a party will be equally impressive. If you wish to make a display for the very first time, and you do not have a container that you like or one that you want to use, try to imagine the sort of arrangement you are trying to create and where you wish to place it in a room. Is it to be on a low table, or a high one, on a shelf, above a mantelpiece? Do you need to make it very tall or to stand on the floor, would you see it from all angles or from one side only? When you have asked yourself these questions, you can formulate some idea of size. Having done this, consider the colours and furnishings in the room. Is there full sunlight or is it a very dark room? If the room is neutral, select your favourite colour and then decide which kind of container would be most appropriate. If you have a rustic home, any sort of container will work, but if you have a very modern house, a rustic basket or terracotta pot may look out of place – so aim for a simple, stylish vase or pottery jug. If this is your first attempt, choose a plain-coloured vase; this enables you to have more fun using a bright array of flowers that will not be overpowered by a busily patterned container.

Basketware
Baskets and dried flowers could have been invented to complement each other! The choice of basket styles has broadened enormously over the past few years. The Philippines has been largely responsible for this increase in style and quality. If you are on holiday, look out for unusual baskets; sadly the large and extremely unusual styles do not always make their way to our shores. If you have a basket that you do not like in its present form, why not spray it a bright colour or match it with your furnishings; this will often kindle the spark of inspiration and bring additional style to a rather uninteresting basket. Since dried flowers weigh so little, a very thin weave basket will do – and steer clear of very large baskets while you are still a novice.

Florists, gift shops and 'ethnic' shops are all good sources of baskets. Hardware stores supply strong shopping baskets and if you are fortunate enough to know a local basket-maker he will probably supply to order.

A versatile selection of containers which includes jugs, teapots, an egg cup, a mustard jar, a ceramic wall hanger, a flowerpot, a jelly mould, as well as classical vases and flower containers in glass and ceramic.

Terracotta

One of our oldest forms of container, and still one of the most popular, is made from terracotta. Dried flowers are particularly appropriate for the rough texture and rustic colour of this type of pottery. Exotica, leaves, natural colours, tougher pods and seed heads are probably the most suitable material to use as they are sympathetic to the 'feel' of the material – but a mass of simple white daisies or a haze of gypsophila can look just as appealing.

If you decide to use a pot that has been outside, make sure it is absolutely dry before using it for your arrangement. Dried flowers hate damp and humid conditions and mildew will form quickly on the lower stalks in a moist atmosphere. For best results, let the pot dry out naturally. I would not place it near direct heat or stand it on a boiler or radiator, this might cause cracks to the surface, making it look unattractive and weakening the container. Terracotta is usually left unglazed, so extra care must be taken.

Commercial potteries have improved the toughness of containers and have ensured a much wider choice of container type. Garden centres stock good ranges as do some hardware stores. Local potteries are a must if you are searching for something slightly more unusual.

Ceramics

The term 'ceramic' encompasses an enormous variety of containers, from vases to gravy boats. Any vase will be suitable, but note that narrow-necked vases can only be used with a few blooms. Many vases are decorated with pretty designs; you could pick out a couple of the predominant colours and find flowers to match. Take it a stage further by matching the arrangement to the colour of the fabric in your room. Avoid pots which are highly glazed or are decorated with overpoweringly gaudy patterns – one quickly loses sight of the subtlety which is the trademark of dried flower arrangements.

Other containers

In this category one's imagination is the best possible accessory. Shown on the previous page are some ideas you might like to try, so look around your house and see what you can find. Coal scuttles are very attractive and, on a smaller scale, so are old teapots or sugar bowls, a pretty mug, a piece of attractive drift wood – the choice is endless.

Opposite
An extraordinary array of baskets from many different countries. Most of the popular shapes for dried flower arranging are shown here.

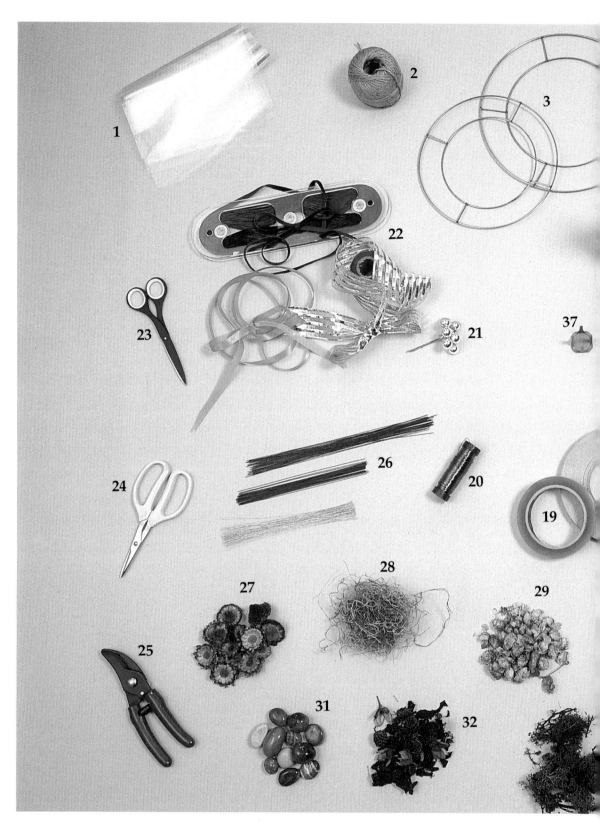

SUNDRIES

There are only three or four important items you will need when making your arrangement, and a few items which will be necessary for making trees, garlands and swags (see Chapter 5). For vases, baskets and containers generally, you will need the items explained in Chapter 3. Most of these accessories can be purchased at a good florists; hardware stores are a good source of secateurs, a sharp steel knife and chicken wire.

1 Cellophane paper
2 Ball of string
3 Wire-frame garland rings
4 Wire netting for covering plastic foam
5 Natural wicker ring for garlands
6 Deep brown wicker ring for garlands
7 Lavender woven heart
8 Oasis block
9 Oasis cone
10 Oasis garland base
11 Small Oasis sphere
12 Medium Oasis sphere
13 Oasis cylinder
14 Terracotta flowerpot
15 Candle-holder
16 Gold candle for festive occasions
17 Clay
18 Florist's tape
19 Transparent sticky tape
20 Reel of wire
21 Small silver baubles for festive decorations
22 Assortment of ribbons
23 Sharp scissors for cutting paper, tapes and ribbons
24 Sharp strong florist's scissors to cut flower stalks
25 Secateurs for tough stems
26 Selection of stub wires of various thicknesses
27 Small cones
28 Tilancia (moss)
29 Hops
30 Fir-cones
31 Polished stones
32 Pot-pourri
33 Moss
34 Flower heads
35 Plaster of Paris
36 Craft knife
37 Flower clip

CHAPTER 3
HOW TO MAKE A BASIC ARRANGEMENT

Opposite above
Bridesmaid's basket

Left
Place the clay or plastic foam in the basket and work in a circular fashion building up height as you add more flowers.

Centre
The base filling is now completed. Notice the spiky effect which is created from leaving gaps in which to put the flowers.

Right
Cut the flowers to the length you require and arrange them in a symmetrical fashion, gradually adding more until you are satisfied with the result. Always use all your stock of one flower type before moving on to another.

Opposite below
Medium-sized pot or basket

Left
Put the clay or plastic foam in the basket, placing the filler, in this case sea lavender, into the base. Gradually build up the shape and height turning the basket frequently to ensure that the pieces are even all round.

Centre
Start to add the flowers, systematically working through the flower types, thus creating different heights.

Right
Gypsophila, when added as a final flourish, creates a hazy effect that contrasts with the sharper shapes of the middle stage.

Arrangements can be made in almost any type of container: baskets, vases, pots, pans, jars, teapots, coal scuttles, to name but a few. Possibly the most difficult container to use is one of very clear glass because, unlike fresh flower stalks which can look very attractive when placed in water, dried flower stalks usually look quite dreadful. The way round this problem is to place some dried plastic foam (Oasis) block in the middle of the container, then fill the glass area with pretty pot-pourri, hop heads, flower heads, fine dry sand or little stones (often available in pet shops), all of which provide weight and a good grip, thus making arranging easier.

Choose a container which is in proportion to the area you wish to decorate and make sure it is not going to overbalance or protrude too far out: for example if you are decorating a narrow sill or shelf. If you are making an arrangement for fun, select a container which is easy to work with, not narrow-necked vases or terribly wide-brimmed baskets. Narrow-necked vases are hard to arrange and you need a good deal of skill and patience to fill wide-brimmed baskets successfully. It is also worth noting that wide-brimmed baskets swallow up a larger amount of flowers.

When you have made your choice, you will need to gather together the following items: your chosen flowers; a plastic foam block or drihard clay; a good pair of scissors or secateurs (paper or nail scissors simply will not do); stubb wires or a reel of wire; a pin to anchor the plastic foam or clay to the bottom of the container and some glue to fix the plastic foam. Lay all these items on a large cloth or newspaper: you are now ready to start.

Place the plastic foam or clay in the container. If you are using plastic foam, stick down the block using a florist's pin secured by glue from a glue gun, use a very strong domestic glue or plastic foam fix.

I generally find clay to be a better alternative to plastic foam, since it gives such excellent stability to the container, especially a lightweight one. It is also a practical medium to work with, being more flexible at the initial stage when you are placing the stalks. A great disadvantage with plastic foam is that it tends to disintegrate, whereas when using clay all you have to do is squeeze it back into shape. The one thing to remember about clay, is that it does dry completely hard within twenty-four to forty-eight hours depending on the room temperature, so if you are dissatisfied with your creation, take it out and start again. Alternatively, put the clay into a tightly sealed, dampened polythene bag until you feel ready to have another go. An advantage of using clay is it is very easy to remove from the container when hard. To save any flowers, simply snip them off as close to the base as possible – it should leave your container only slightly dusty and therefore immediately reusable.

The helpful thing about working with plastic foam is that there is no in-built time limit you can simply pull all the flowers out, and take days to arrange them if you wish! It is important to remember that there is special plastic foam for dried flowers. Plastic foam for fresh flowers or 'wet plastic foam', only works in water and is therefore inappropriate.

Take the first bunch of flowers you wish to arrange and sort them into the required lengths. A good tip is always to snip a little piece off the end irrespective of the length required, this will ensure that the stalks sink more readily into the base. Strip off any crumbly leaves and excess side stalks that will catch on other stems as you place them in the container.

These three different sorts of popular container demonstrate basic arranging techniques pertinent to the heights and widths of any other type of container you might use:

1 An oval bridesmaid's basket with handle over.
2 A round, medium height and width pot or basket.
3 A tall vase.

Shape is all important to any arrangement, so try to visualize the end result before you start. There is always the danger of creating a large, amorphous arrangement by accident.

1 BRIDESMAID'S OR NELL GWYN BASKET

These extremely popular baskets are, just as their name suggests, *de rigueur* at weddings. Usually carried by the bridesmaid, they are often characterized by pretty ribbons trailing down the side (see Chapter 8).

Method
Place the clay or plastic foam (Oasis) in the centre of the basket and arrange equal lengths of one type of base flower (such as sea lavender or grasses) evenly, so that you form a perfectly even outer circle. Keep the stems fairly flat to the basket, all hanging slightly over the brim, to break up the hard edge of the basket. They should protrude about one inch all round unless you wish to have a more trailing effect, then you should allow lengths of about three inches to hang over each end.

Put the next row in position, still working in a circle, but this time put the stems in at a slight upward angle. Continue arranging the flowers in a circular design until the basket is filled.

Now take a second type of flower, preferably a completely different shape and place the florets quite geometrically at first until approximately six spaces have been evenly filled. Continue with a third type filling in the spaces between the flowers already in position. Three varieties are an ideal balance for any basket, but if you have more, the different shapes will only improve the overall effect.

2 A ROUND POT OR BASKET

The rules for this design are virtually identical to those which apply to (1) above. There are, however, two small variations: there is no handle to incorporate into the design; and you have the choice of creating an all-round look or a flat-backed arrangement. If the choice is to be an all-round design, place the first flowers in

the basket as in (1) above, keeping a perfect round with the same lengths of flowers. Then, depending on the height you wish to achieve, start to build up the circle working towards the middle. Having used a base flower, repeat the method which applied to the bridesmaid's basket, only varying the lengths to match the height of the container.

3 A TALL VASE

Vases vary enormously in shape, but the same rule applies: the height of the arrangement should not exceed more than twice the height of the vase, unless the vase is particularly large and the space you wish to fill is very high, for example a very big fireplace. Try to judge the height and width accordingly, for if ignored the whole thing quickly becomes out of proportion. Begin by placing the highest, most spiky plants in the vase, forming a rough triangular shape. The second type of flower should fill the spaces between the first variety used. Continue to fill the spaces until you have hidden the clay or plastic foam and the display has finally taken on the shape you desire. You could perhaps finish this arrangement off with something soft such as gypsophila, alchemilla or a shimmery grass such as briza (quaking grass) – depending of course, on the size of the gaps that remain and the style you wish to create.

Vase

Place the larkspur in the vase to create the height and shape you require, then add the sea lavender between the pieces, building up a triangular shape to the back and sides.

Opposite
Taking one type of flower at a time, aim for a contrast in both colour and flower type. Here I have used caspia, larkspur, achillea, statice, poppy heads, cream helichrysum, matecaria and gypsophila.

WIRING

Wiring flowers is not as difficult or time consuming as it may appear; it does, however, require patience and gentle hands. Most flowers can be supported in clusters with wires, or a wire pushed through the head will hold it firmly in place. Stalks that have been dried are often flimsy, hard and brittle. The heads of roses, helichrysum and peonies are large enough to withstand a wire placed directly into the flower head. Other flowers, leaves or cones have to be supported in other ways, often by strengthening the existing stem. Hydrangea and honesty can be wired by threading the wire through underneath the heads onto the fragile smaller stems, then back down onto the main stalk. Now the flowers can be wired *en masse* onto a thicker wire which will give greater flexibility when they are to form part of an arrangement.

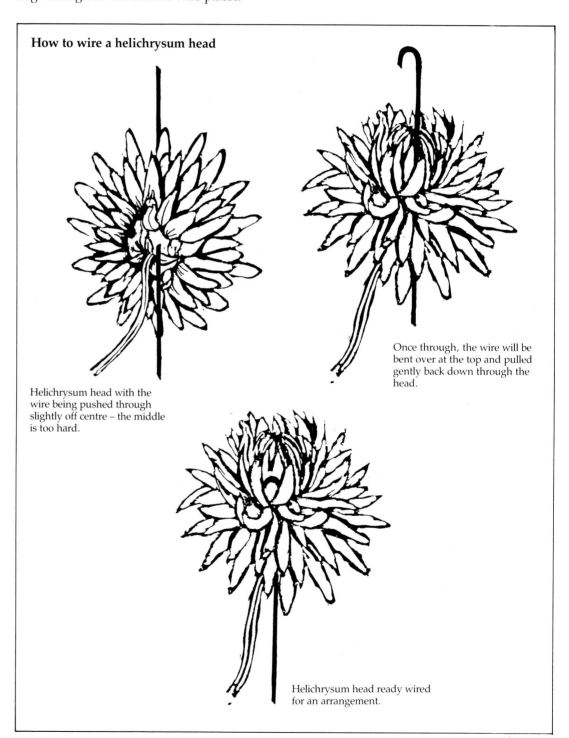

How to wire a helichrysum head

Helichrysum head with the wire being pushed through slightly off centre – the middle is too hard.

Once through, the wire will be bent over at the top and pulled gently back down through the head.

Helichrysum head ready wired for an arrangement.

How to wire a rose head

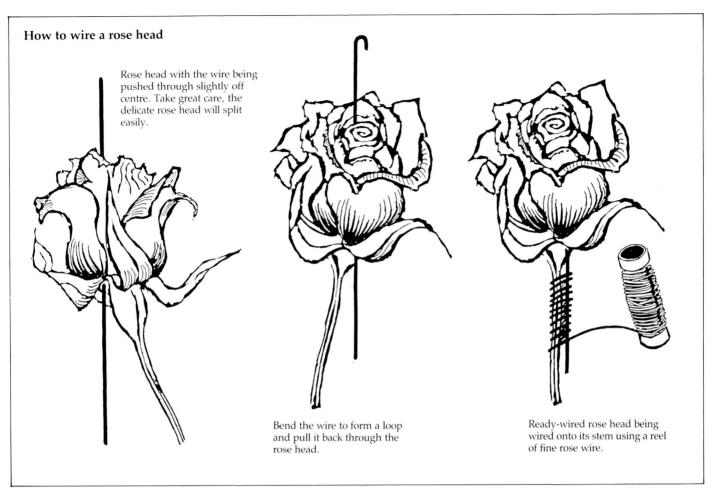

Rose head with the wire being pushed through slightly off centre. Take great care, the delicate rose head will split easily.

Bend the wire to form a loop and pull it back through the rose head.

Ready-wired rose head being wired onto its stem using a reel of fine rose wire.

Wiring a cluster of flowers

This group of flowers is being wired for an arrangement, swag, tree or garland.

Wiring a fir-cone

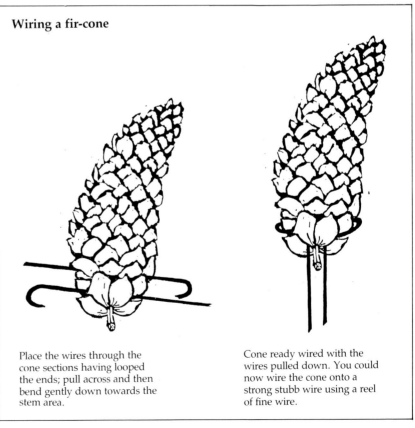

Place the wires through the cone sections having looped the ends; pull across and then bend gently down towards the stem area.

Cone ready wired with the wires pulled down. You could now wire the cone onto a strong stubb wire using a reel of fine wire.

CHAPTER 4
PRINCIPAL TYPES
OF ARRANGEMENTS

GEORGIAN FIREPLACE DISPLAY

Georgian, grey-marble town
house fireplace display in a red
and black stained rattan
basket, filled with red
sterlingia and lagurus.

FIREPLACES

Fireplaces are the focal point of many of our homes, and one of the loveliest ways to fill that dark gap is with a dried flower arrangement. If the fireplace is purely ornamental, or perhaps in a spare room, you could try different displays to suit the seasons, always taking care to match some facet of your room decor. If you use your fire in the winter months, the splash of colour from an arrangement provides a lovely contrast throughout the summer. Always remember, however, to stuff some newspaper up the chimney before putting the arrangement in place: many glorious displays have been spoilt by an untimely soot fall!

To make fireplace displays, you generally need a good deal of flowers, both in terms of variety and quantity. It is worth remembering that the arrangement will be seen from above as well as from the sides and front so try to keep it 'full'. Usually these displays are flat-backed but you may like to make an arrangement that you can turn around should one side begin to look a bit faded.

Things you will need:
1 As many types and shapes of dried flowers as possible.
2 Any container appropriate to the style of room (eg brass coal scuttle for a farmhouse living-room or a chic vase for a modern drawing-room).
3 Drihard clay or plastic foam if the container will be needed again.
4 Wires, scissors and enough space to lay out all your flowers before making the arrangement.

BASIC METHOD

Measure the space you want to fill and methodically lay all the flowers on an old sheet or newspaper (cloth is generally better, because when you have finished arranging you can pick the whole thing up and empty it outside). Having done this, place the clay or plastic foam in your chosen container, then work out which flowers will form the height and shape, always work with one type of flower at a time. If any of the bunches have heavy seed heads or very thick stems, try to place these early on as they will tend to pull down and damage gentler blooms, such as gypsophila, which should really be placed in last of all – they are useful for filling holes and creating a soft hazy look.

The basic rules for dried flower arranging are very simple. The main points to consider are:

1 Do you want the arrangement to blend in with the decor, highlight a particular colour in the room, or to clash slightly? The latter can be very effective, if cleverly done.
2 The type of container you choose is very important, it should neither be so grand as to overshadow the display, nor so small as to fade into insignificance. Remember that it is part of the overall 'look' of the arrangement. Very often the ideal receptacle is in the room already. Perhaps a little-used vase, basket or even a terracotta flowerpot? Some fireplaces need nothing at all – simply make the arrangement in the grate, or allow a cascade of flowers to pour out of the open doors of a woodburning stove.
3 Finally, having decided upon the colour scheme and container, consider carefully the shape and style you are trying to achieve.
a) Shape: should it be a spiky or cushion effect, flat-backed or all-round look?
b) Style: formal or informal, controlled or wild?

When you have decided upon the shape and style of your arrangement you are ready to begin. The following paragraphs deal with most types of fireplace design and suggest appropriate dried flower displays.

GEORGIAN

Beautifully proportioned Georgian houses usually have fireplaces to match and allow you plenty of scope to create an impressive display. Often the actual aperture is quite large and the surround is in marble backed by grey stone. Whatever type of arrangement you choose to create, make sure that the proportions are as near perfect as possible. The most effective, I find, are flat-backed-type basket displays, with a minimum depth of eight inches; or a smart vase, round enough to set off the width of the fireplace, in either ceramic or marble.

VICTORIAN

Many Victorian fireplaces are quite small and tiled with a decorative cast-iron surround. They do not have particularly large apertures and do not need huge arrangements – very often a mass of flowers placed directly into the grate will suffice. For practical reasons, particularly when the fireplace is in constant use, a small vase or basket arrangement is better. It is important not to hide the generally

VICTORIAN FIREPLACE DISPLAY

COUNTRY HOUSE FIREPLACE DISPLAY

A small country-house fireplace in green marble with a wood surround. This rustic display in warm autumn colours is placed in a heavy wicker shopping basket showing a mixture of large fir-cones, preserved oak and beech leaves, carthamus, morrison, basilia, *Dryandra formosa* and apricot African everlasting daisies.

Opposite
This Victorian fireplace is brought to life with a country display in a blue pot-shaped glazed terracotta vase. It is filled with pink larkspur, pink and white rhodanthe daisies, red bonnie and matecaria.

FARMHOUSE FIREPLACE DISPLAY

This farmhouse fireplace contains a mass of warmly glowing Chinese lanterns, pittosporum and beech leaves in an attractive surround. The display is placed in a green matt, gold-flecked classic vase, standing on a terracotta brick floor.

attractive surround or swamp the area with something too large. Soft flowers such as daisies, larkspurs, nigella and a touch of gypsophila lend themselves to the Victorian period.

COUNTRY HOUSE/MANOR HOUSE

Fireplaces in large country houses tend to be of the dimensions which really do justice to extravagant displays. If your home sits in mature grounds, with interesting plants and shrubs, take large cuttings – such as hemlock, beech or oak leaves – dry or glycerine them and place them in terracotta urns, marble cache pots or pots on pedestals. If this is not your style why not go for a very big log basket crammed full of all sorts of grasses and flowers; the basket of flowers can be created from many varieties to suit your furnishings.

FARMHOUSE

Farmhouses generally have a cosy intimate feel, and their chimney places are equally warm and friendly. The fireplace is often the focal point of the room in these lovely buildings, whether it be a brick construction or a woodburner. Often these red-brick fireplaces are quite large with logs stacked nearby – so the overall atmosphere of the arrangement should be both warm and vibrant to complement the room. Formal or informal, choose your mood, whilst keeping the display well proportioned. Often the arrangement looks good in a brass coal scuttle, small log basket or terracotta pot; these types of fireplaces also look wonderful at Christmas time adorned with swags and garlands.

MODERN

There is a very wide variety of modern fireplaces, and thus they are harder to define as a 'type'. European ones tend to be stone built or modern brick, whereas North American examples are often of wood surround. A principal rule is to keep the arrangement in proportion to the aperture while remembering that understatement is usually safer when using dried flowers. If you have a very modern room, a stark, spray-painted arrangement can look very dramatic. Sometimes these fireplaces incorporate little niches – fill these with a small bunch of flowers, or perhaps a tiny basket arrangement, but try to keep these pretty yet discreet.

MANTELPIECES

To finish off the arrangement, you may want to place a small display on the mantelpiece to counterbalance it. Generally, perhaps with the exception of modern fireplaces, these are unlikely to be less than 4ft 6in from the ground, and are often substantially higher. The one thing to avoid is being able to see a lot of stalks and the underside of the flower heads. A good tip is to keep placing the arrangement in its final position while you are working on it. Round-headed flowers, such as daisy types, small clusters and foliage are ideal for this type of design (see Chapter 2). The effect should not be overpowering, especially if there is an arrangement in the hearth as well. The position of these arrangements depends on the shape and height – the trick is to achieve a 'balance'. An effective alternative is to choose a basket or container that can be tilted with its arrangement on the mantelpiece, so that all you see is the top of the display. Swags, too, look gorgeous laid simply across or pinned to the mantel – when you are having a party you might add a couple of candlesticks with candle colours to match the flowers. Take care not to put the candles close to the flowers.

TABLE DISPLAYS

Table displays are probably my favourite area of dried flower arranging, the possibilities are endless and there are few rules to follow. Most people will welcome a display that does not have to be changed, particularly during the winter months when fresh flowers are expensive and, unless you live in a large town, the choice is frequently limited.

Wherever you choose to make your display, the size of the arrangement in proportion to the area where it is to be placed must be considered. The arrangement must not overpower the table, nor should it hang over the edge unless it is positioned well away from danger. Dried flowers are best positioned in the centre of a table or made into a flat-backed display to be placed against a wall, such as on a hall table.

CENTRAL DISPLAYS

These are extremely popular and look attractive in many sorts of surroundings. Dining tables and coffee tables are popular and although both types are central, they require a completely different treatment.

They both have to be made in an all-round

MANTELPIECE DISPLAY

shape but vary in as much as the low coffee table will be seen mainly from above while the dining table, although seen from above, will generally be seen at eye level. If the arrangement is not sufficiently 'filled' the rather ugly central plastic foam will be visible; it is a most unattractive sight and ruins the arrangement. Make sure that you have enough filling materials to hand, sea lavender or moss are ideal. A display on a low table should not be so large that it dominates the space – it should sit in place quite comfortably, in proportion to the other articles that may surround it. Dining-table displays should be attractive but not too overpowering; an arrangement that is too large will monopolize the available space and also obstruct visibility between your family or guests! If you are making place settings, keep them small: remember that you may have two or three sets of glasses at a formal occasion. Tiny baskets or posies are best. If you are making a display involving candles, do ensure that the flowers are kept fairly short and the candles are non-drip.

When you are seated at table you are seeing the arrangement from a completely different perspective and it is important that you are not faced with a multitude of stems. Try to bring the flowers down to the edge of the container, thereby softening the general appearance. Generally, a low-spreading central arrangement is best, particularly if you have a long table to decorate. A very good method is to make a display on a low block of plastic foam or on a piece of wood which will sit directly onto the table. To prevent it from slipping or scratching the surface, cut out a piece of felt or cork and stick it to the bottom.

If you are making a display for the kitchen table, make sure that it is relatively unobtrusive, and can be easily removed if you want to use the table as a work-top. In the kitchen an upright vase or well-balanced flat-bottomed basket are best, as this tends to be such a busy place. (For the basic instruction on making an all-round arrangement, see Chapter 3.)

FLAT-BACKED DISPLAYS

These are very pleasing arrangements and usually quite simple to make. Try mixing the colours so that the display will suit more than one area in your home. Hall tables and side tables are appropriate subjects; remember to keep the size of your arrangement in proportion to the surface area. Hallways are generally very busy, so ensure that the container will support the flowers properly and that children and pets thundering past cannot do any damage. Choose, where possible, slightly more robust flowers which are not so greatly affected by draughts – flowers such as poppy heads and seed heads, leaves, sea holly, kangaroo paw, bottle brush, grasses and Chinese lanterns are hardy varieties. The display itself will be seen from three sides, so consider the side views as well, they are often forgotten.

A huge quantity of grasses is appropriate in a floor display, try to place it where it will catch the odd ray of sunlight. Grasses are the least affected by direct sunlight because they are naturally a neutral, rather bleached colour. They are also very sturdy and will cope with being at some height from the floor.

Other popular flat-backed displays are hanging wall baskets or flat-backed terracotta containers. These are incredibly useful where surface space is limited or unsuitable, for example in a narrow corridor or a bathroom. Wall containers should not be too high. Unlike fresh flowers, dried flowers are generally rigid and do not hang naturally or trail over the edges of the containers – this can be overcome by wiring flowers together and placing them at an angle, but avoid the 'unnatural' look, try layering them to create a better effect (grasses, ferns, sea lavender and leaves are useful for this purpose). Ideally, the arrangement should be at eye level. If you do, however, choose to make one that is above eye level, place it in position from time to time to make sure that you are creating the right effect.

Most houses have small, hidden nooks and crannies where it is too dark to take fresh flowers or house plants. These are perfect surroundings for dried flowers. Check the size and create a display in proportion to the area. Make sure that the position is not damp and that the flowers will not be affected by any rising steam or great heat.

HANGING BASKETS, BUNCHES AND BOUQUETS

Hanging baskets are similar to wall displays to make since they are frequently hung higher than eye level. They are usually seen from all

Wedgwood blue walls surrounding an extraordinary baroque fireplace provide the perfect setting for a mantelpiece display within the little alcove. The turfo pot contains creamy yellow roses, blue ti-tree, white ti-tree, sea holly, achillea 'pearl' and gypsophila.

round, in a stairwell for instance. The easiest way to make this arrangement is while it is hanging *in situ*. Find an open area where you can place a hook and hang it so that it is just above your work surface. Rotate the basket while it is being worked on to ensure that it is well balanced. To obtain a trailing effect, follow the instructions for wall baskets, in this chapter.

You may not have a suitable space to hang a suspended basket, in which case you could hang bunches from beams, or in the corner of a room. Try placing bunches on top of a cupboard that looks rather bare; place them in layers with the heads poking over the edge – this can be so effective. Choose flowers that complement the surroundings and pick colours that match the decor.

This simple black modern fireplace, and an equally stark black vase, accentuates a mass of white acroclinium daisies.

BUNCHES AND BOUQUETS IN CORNERS

These are pretty, simple to create, and can be the perfect solution if guests arrive suddenly and you have had no time to make a flower display for their room. Place one, two or three bunches together, tie them securely, place a hook or small nail in the corner of the room and suspend the bunch from the nail. Add a matching ribbon, or alternatively attach the bunch to the nail with raffia for a more rustic look. These bunches can be placed anywhere in the house, and are wonderful if you are short of surface space.

MODERN FIREPLACE DISPLAY

HANGING FLOWERS

Single bunches of flowers are a traditional way of decorating beams in kitchens, this is not only an ideal way of drying the flowers but is also extemely decorative. Do not limit them to the kitchen – be adventurous throughout the house.

Bouquets made from these flowers make perfect gifts, they also look nice on the wall in the same way as you would hang a picture. Make the bouquet flat-backed, spreading the flowers out to form a fan-shaped display. Put the flowers on the table, placing the longest ones down first, then the next layer and so on. As a final touch tie the stems together with satin ribbons – use two colours from your choice of flowers to enhance the overall effect.

Flat-backed hanging basket on a pine door. I have used adiantum, pink phalaris, alchemilla, lilac statice, gypsophila, sea lavender and hydrangea.

FLAT-BACKED DISPLAY

FLAT-BACKED DISPLAY

Flat-backed wall display in a
Scottish broom basket
containing a simple
arrangement of oak leaves,
pittosporum, yellow roses and
flax.

Opposite

Wall bouquet made with an
extraordinarily rich mix of
colours and flower types
including chrysanthemum,
cockscomb, hydrangea,
nigella, roses, alchemilla,
lipidium, oats, polypogon and
gypsophila.

WALL DISPLAY

KITCHEN DISPLAY

Farmhouse kitchen table display – sufficiently versatile to be used elsewhere when the table is in use. A small rustic country shopping basket is filled with hydrangea, amaranthus, statice, larkspur, roses and gypsophila.

TABLE DISPLAY

This tasteful entrance hall table display blends impeccably with its surroundings. The white glazed plant-pot holder with gold edging contains cream larkspur, achillea 'pearl', helichrysum, white baby star and sea lavender.

Opposite

Wood panelling is the perfect background for this sophisticated display. The plain white vase contains pink roses, hydrangea, lipidium grass and eucalyptus.

TABLE DISPLAY

A DISPLAY FOR NOOKS AND CRANNIES

Nooks and crannies can be very successfully filled with small containers of different flowers. Here the main feature is an attractive white teapot filled with red bonnie and lilac statice. Red roses, hydrangea, white rhodanthe daisies, quaking grass, oats, poppy heads and amaranthus fill the other corner gaps.

FLOOR DISPLAY

Impressively catching the
sunlight is this tall, grey-
marble vase with a mass of
transparent honesty.

STAIRWELL DISPLAY

Grand autumn stairwell display. Stone antique font-type container with beech leaves, oak and pittosporum leaves, hydrangea, kangaroo paw, helichrysum, matecaria, achillea 'moonshine', achillea 'pearl', nigella, white larkspur, gypsophila, sterlingia, centaurea, eucalyptus and cones.

FLOOR DISPLAY

Ultra-modern floor display at
the foot of the staircase
containing a mass of pink
rhodanthe daisies.

SHELF DISPLAY

Shelf display on a dresser,
picking out the gentle colours
of the crockery. Sea lavender,
phalaris, everlasting daisies,
pink roses, lipidium, baby star,
sea holly and curry flower.

TABLE DISPLAY

Oriental dining-room display.
Pink eucalyptus and curly
grass on a black marble table.

SHELF DISPLAY

TABLE DISPLAY

Old-fashioned floral wallpaper in softly muted colours complements the stronger shades of the arrangement. An ancient terracotta pot is filled with hydrangea, caspia, larkspur, love-lies-bleeding, monkshood, sea holly, matecaria, achillea 'moonshine' and lemon-tinted helichrysum.

Exquisitely chic side-table display in a plain white vase containing eucalyptus, pink roses and the lightest touch of gypsophila.

SHELF DISPLAY

Narrow shelf nook with a white boat-shaped vase containing a thick cluster of hydrangea heads in muted pinks and greens. This arrangement contrasts with the depth of colour in the walls.

Opposite
This elegant hall-table display in a simple white porcelain jug contains golden achillea, pink larkspur, pink helichrysum, pink rhodanthe, deep red peonies, pink peonies and gypsophila.

TABLE DISPLAY

SHELF DISPLAY

Natural sunlight provides
delicate illumination for this
pretty camomile-woven basket
filled with a mass of flax.

SHELF DISPLAY

One can sense the scents of summer from this window-seat arrangement that discreetly echoes the curtain fabric colours and blends with the greenery in the garden. This bleached wicker bread basket is ideal for a long window seat and is filled with pink *Verticordia brownii*, ti-tree, peonies, cockscomb, adiantum fern, eucalyptus, phalaris, larkspur, pink helichrysum, white *Helichrysum vestium*, hydrangea, broom bloom and gypsophila.

TABLE DISPLAY

This informal dining table is home to an arrangement that matches the crockery. Monkshood, amaranthus, hydrangea, nigella, matecaria, and creamy yellow roses combine to make a colourful all-year-round display.

CHAPTER 5
TREES, GARLANDS AND SWAGS

This pom-pom tree blends perfectly with the pale grey decor and hand-painted pink rose stencils. The pink rhodanthe daisies, gomphrena, white baby star, pink roses, and ti-tree are mounted on a medium-sized plastic foam ball filled with a sea lavender and caspia base.

The trunk is bound with pink satin ribbon tied neatly within the flowers to hide the knot. Satin bows surrounding the pom-pom are a nice finishing touch.

TREES

Pom-pom and conical trees

Making dried flower trees might appear to be a rather awesome undertaking, particularly if you are just a beginner. Take heart, it is quite a simple procedure, and the end result is usually very satisfying.

Do not try to make too big a tree on your first attempt – try a table tree. The same method applies to all sizes of tree, but obviously you will use far more flowers, wires and general bits and pieces for the bigger displays. It makes economic sense, therefore, to use as much material from your garden as possible.

Hydrangea heads are wonderful for this arrangement as they can be used in their entirety to form the round or the conical shape. Some look so pretty, you need not add much more than a few ribbons, or maybe something fluffy and hazey like alchemilla or gypsophila to contrast with the large florets of the hydrangea.

Another excellent base is sea lavender, the white rather stiff little flowers are perfect for holding flowers subsequently placed in the display.

Large pom-pom trees can look very impressive either side of a wide staircase, especially if the stairs are complemented by a large entrance hall. It is important to position this arrangement where it will be safe. The fragile head will easily spoil and hours of work would be needlessly ruined. Avoid direct sunlight: if this is difficult, restrict yourself to one light colour, using many different flower types. For example, try a white and cream arrangement using cream helichrysum, achillea 'pearl', *Helichrysum vestium*, cream larkspur, cream baby star and gypsophila.

Left
Sea lavender based pom-pom tree with pink roses and their leaves, hydrangea, lilac achillea, larkspur and white *Helichrysum vestium*, in a white ceramic pot filled with moss.

Centre
Conical tree made with pittosporum leaves and adiantum on a moss-covered plastic foam base, placed in a terracotta flowerpot.

Right
Pom-pom tree with no filler base. It is made with a mass of hydrangea, roses, baby star, lipidium and gypsophila and sunk into a basket and surrounded with tilancia. A pink, satin ribbon bow tied to the pom-pom completes the arrangement.

HOW TO MAKE POM-POM OR CONICAL TREES

Materials required

1. A plastic foam ball (Oasis), cone or block (if you use a block, you will have to cut it to the required shape, using a sharp craft knife).
2. Fine mesh chicken wire and wire cutters.
3. A stave, pole or branch for the trunk and a small saw.
4. A reel of wire and stubb wires.
5. Flowerpot or container of your choice.
6. Plaster of Paris, or similar filler and some water.
7. Glue.
8. Moss or stones to cover the plaster of Paris.
9. Strong florist's scissors or secateurs.
10. The flowers.

It is advisable to complete the basic stages in an area where you have ample space and that this area is protected by newspaper or an old sheet. The most important factor is to determine the required height of the finished tree: remember, the height of the flowers placed into the top of the plastic foam will be its finished height. Be warned, unless you are careful, they always end up taller than you originally intended. Try to be as methodical as possible. First, cut the stave, pole or branch to the length of your choice. Mix the plaster of Paris, following carefully the instructions on the packet, remember that it dries extremely quickly. This can be an advantage, because you can complete the tree within the day; whereas if you are using cement or household fillers they take longer and should be prepared the day before.

Put some plaster of Paris in the pot (a plastic flowerpot is the most suitable container), leaving at least half an inch of space from the rim (this is to make room for moss, cones or other material which will hide the filler). Then push the pole down to the bottom of the pot, do not push too quickly, or plaster will burst over the edge onto the floor. Hold the pole in position for a couple of minutes, step back and make sure it is straight. Allow the plaster of Paris to set completely before the next stage. The flowerpot can be placed in a basket, ceramic pot, terracotta urn, brass coal scuttle – in fact whatever you choose to suite the room. Any plaster of Paris that has marked the stave or the containers can be wiped off with a warm damp cloth.

Place the plastic foam you have chosen onto the stave and, making sure that it is in a central position, push it down quite hard so that the pole goes through about half-way. Be very careful not to push so hard that the pole comes out of the other side. Pull the plastic foam out, brush off the top of the pole and apply a generous amount of strong adhesive. Then put the plastic foam back again, hold it in place for a moment, then release. Now allow it to dry.

Cut the chicken wire to fit the plastic foam and, letting the wire suspend from the base of the plastic foam, pull it together, bunching it underneath. Taking the reel of wire, unravel enough to enable you to thread the wire through the mesh (fig 1). Gather it in under the base of the plastic foam and bend it until it is all neatly tucked away; then pull the wire together, secure it by twisting the ends, and snip off any unwanted bits. Cover any sharp ends with strong tape. Be careful not to tape too far down the stave as this may show below the flower level.

As I mentioned above, one of the most popular bases for covering the plastic foam is sea lavender. It is economical as it covers a large area quickly and forms a solid base. Cut the sea lavender into equal lengths of your choice before you begin. Working methodically, place all the sea lavender in the plastic foam, making sure the balance is correct on all sides, whether the shape is round or conical (fig 2). The overall style of the arrangement will be determined by personal preference. Some people like a smooth, flat cushion-like base, others a more wild, spiky effect. Whatever the end result you can always trim the sea lavender afterwards, turning the tree slowly to ensure that you cut to shape.

If you are only adding leaves, use rather less sea lavender than normal, leaving room for the more bulky stalks of stems and twigs (fig 3). If you have chosen a moss base, place the moss onto the plastic foam shape and secure it with pieces of wire bent into a 'U' shape – wire is more effective than glue. If you are buying sea lavender, a florist will probably recommend about two to three good-sized bunches for a small table tree, and anything up to fifteen bunches for a substantially larger one.

When you have completed the base covering, the flowers you add to the display will hold each other in position. Add colours and shapes that harmonize or contrast. Try wiring bunches of one type together to form a large bright cluster: perhaps some helichrysum heads, different types of daisies, some bobbly broom bloom or hydrangea florets – all these

How to make a conical tree

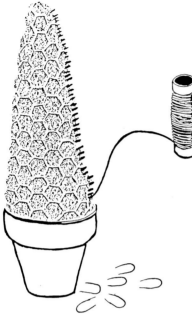

Fig 1: Having secured the plastic foam to the pot using strong glue, encircle the tree with wire netting, and join one side together using the reel of wire.

Fig 2: Attach the moss to the tree using 'U'-shaped pieces of wire.

Fig 3: When you have placed moss all over the base, apply the plant material you have chosen until it is completely covered. When the plastic foam base is covered with moss arrange the plant material so that no part of the base is visible.

How to make a pom-pom tree

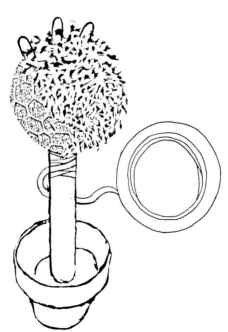

Fig 1: Put the trunk in the pot with the filler and encase the sphere in wire netting. The netting should be secured at the base.

Fig 2: Tape round the wire to mask out sharp edges. Stick the moss or sea lavender into the base; if you use moss, use 'U'-shaped pieces of wire to secure it to the sphere.

Fig 3: Attach the flower material to the tree until the ball takes shape. The tape should not protrude below the level of the flower.

flowers are impressive when used together.

If you have chosen an autumnal theme, yellow achillea heads, morrison or large exotica heads provide an excellent splash of colour; add them to fir-cones, seed pods and a little foliage and the result will be very pleasing. If you want the tree to look feminine, add a bow or some trailing ribbons as a final touch. These usually look best on a pom-pom tree, but little bows placed all round a conical tree can look very pretty.

Conical trees do not have to have a trunk. Using a very efficient adhesive, you could stick the plastic foam cone directly onto the pot, first pushing it down so the cone sits just inside the pot. Naturally, if you are making a large tree, you will be shaping blocks to form the tree, but you can still stick them to the pot. There are glues especially made for this purpose. I also find it easier, when using a cone, to snip off the very top of the cone before using the wire: it is then easier to make the point for the top of the tree.

If you have made your tree with care and attention it should look attractive for years. If you get bored with your choice of flowers, take all the material out, leaving the base covering, and choose a new colour theme. It is possible to do this several times before the plastic foam wears out.

GARLANDS

A garland or wreath is a ring adorned with flowers, leaves, nuts, berries and herbs. They are usually associated with Christmas, and are often seen graciously hanging from front doors. However, with the increasing popularity, and wonderful variety, of dried flowers now available, a garland can be made at any time of the year and become a permanent feature on an inside door, wall or over an archway. They are an attractive alternative to a conventional flower arrangement and, as with all wall-suspended arrangements, are especially appropriate when there is no space to put a vase. They are extremely pretty when hung from bedroom doors, and make excellent birthday presents. They can, of course, be made as a decorative accompaniment to any of our festive occasions, such as Easter. Thanksgiving or Harvest Festival. They make excellent wedding gifts or as an adornment to a pew end (see Chapter 8). Garlands are relatively uncomplicated to make, and there are various bases from which to choose.

HOW TO MAKE A GARLAND

Materials required
1 A wire base, wicker base, moss, straw- or rope-base ring.
2 A reel of wire and stubb wires.
3 Ribbons (optional).
4 Sellotape (for fragile stems).
5 Strong florist's scissors.

First, choose your base. If you are working with a wire-framed ring, the first stage is to encase it with Scotch moss, or simply wire on sea lavender, grasses, lipidium or similar such base plant that would complement the chosen colours. Make clusters of your chosen plant and wire them together and then onto the frame (figs 1 & 2).

Attach the flowers to the base using a reel of wire (or individual wires). Work in a circular fashion, as if making a Catherine wheel. When you have covered the base, check the density; add another group of clusters where you feel it necessary to fill in gaps, or to extend the width of the garland. When you are satisfied with the shape, prepare the second type of flowers you wish to place in the garland. The clusters should be made in exactly the same way, then wired with the base. Try a combination of leaves, caspia, white acroclinium daisies, yellow glixia, achillea 'pearl'; or a mixture of nigella bloom, sea holly, oats, white *Helichrysum vestium* and cream broom bloom to form the backing. These simple combinations are based on colour themes. For an autumnal look, use fir-cones, orange flowers, some beech leaves or pittosporum, add fresh bay leaves which will dry on the ring. Raffia bows hanging casually from both sides complete the display. The choice of colours and shapes will depend on the surrounding decor and the availability of the flowers. When you have completed the round, attach a ribbon or raffia threads at the back to form a loop from which it will hang.

If you are using a ready-made wicker garland the process will be much quicker and generally easier (fig 3). You make the clusters in the same way and attach them to the wicker ring using individual stubb wires. You can complete the circle or form a crescent. Wicker rings are versatile and robust. They can be used with fresh flowers, or holly and pine at Christmas time for an outside garland. Bows and ribbons not only complement the arrangement, but are useful tools for covering any unsightly wire ends.

Opposite
Top
The garland is made from a wire frame encircled with lipidium bunches and decorated with pink roses, lavender, achillea 'pearl' and lilac achillea. Finally, it is tied with a pink satin ribbon.

Bottom left
This garland is made in the same way. Woven in small clusters are red bonnie, nigella, ti-tree and ambrociana – all tied with a pink satin ribbon.

Bottom right
Pieces of hydrangea, cream helichrysum, dill, blue hill flower, nigella, bloom flowers and cream broom bloom form the basis of this garland. A cream satin ribbon completes the effect.

How to make a garland

Fig 1

Make up the flower clusters by binding them with wire.

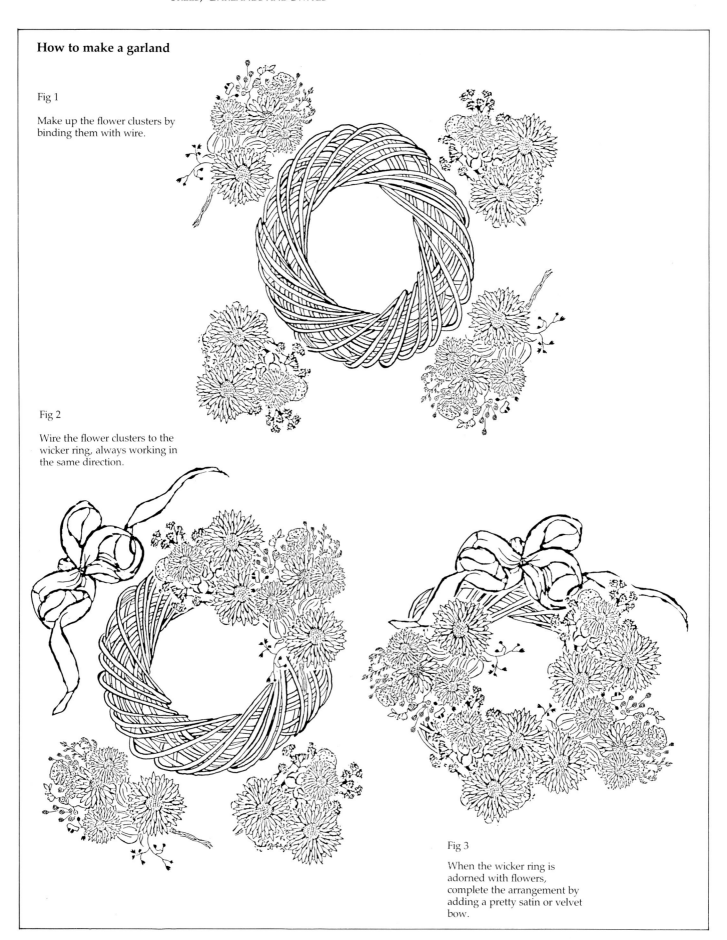

Fig 2

Wire the flower clusters to the wicker ring, always working in the same direction.

Fig 3

When the wicker ring is adorned with flowers, complete the arrangement by adding a pretty satin or velvet bow.

For a different effect try using fir-cones, seed heads and beech nuts instead of flowers. Wire in aniseed stars, cinnamon sticks and fresh herbs such as bay, rosemary and thyme to a kitchen garland.

At Easter time, bind yellow flowers and preserved greenery to a green-rope ring. Add little yellow chicks and sugar eggs, place a candlestick in the middle and you have a charming table centre at Easter. There are so many ideas, take your time experimenting and consider the effect you wish to achieve.

SWAGS

Swags are lengths of cord, moss-covered rope, or wire covered in flowers and hung across an area of your choice. They are favourite forms of decoration at weddings, and add a special touch of originality to an occasion. Swags are frequently made with fresh flowers, but obviously these have a short life span; swags made with dried flowers can be preserved for many years. They take time and patience to make, but the end result is very rewarding and well worth the effort.

HOW TO MAKE A SWAG

Materials required
1 A length of rope, cord or plaited ribbons.
2 Moss (optional).
3 A reel of wire and stubb wires.
4 Strong scissors or secateurs and wire cutters.
5 Ribbons and bows (optional)
6 The flowers.

Begin by measuring the area where the swag will hang. The method of attaching the swag will depend on the surrounding material; if it is marble or stone appropriate attachments will be necessary. If the mantel is very low to the hearth surround, do not let the swag drop beneath it, thus causing a fire hazard. Swags look very attractive lying across the mantelshelf, or placed in the centre of a long dining table. If a candlestick is placed at each end the result is an unusual and unobtrusive

Pretty swags in striking colours ready to hang over a doorway, on a banister or over a fireplace.

85

How to make a swag

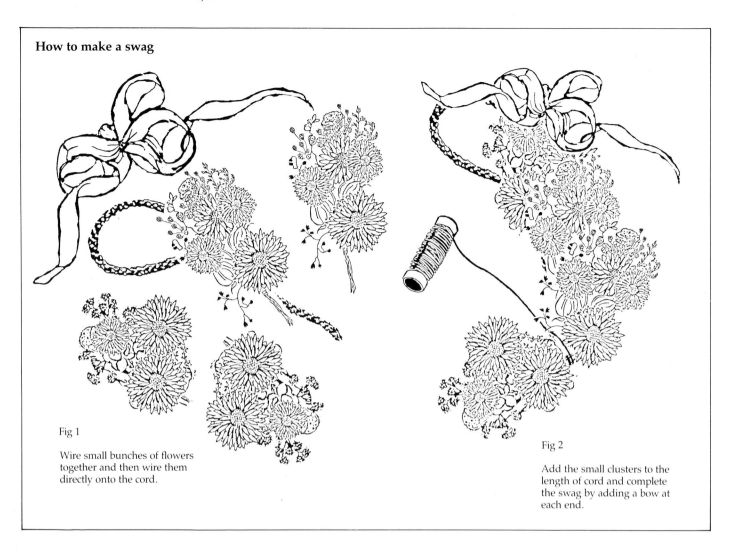

Fig 1

Wire small bunches of flowers together and then wire them directly onto the cord.

Fig 2

Add the small clusters to the length of cord and complete the swag by adding a bow at each end.

table setting. Swags used in this way are particularly appropriate for banquets or wedding breakfasts.

Having decided where you will place the swag, tie a loop at each end or make the necessary provisions for hanging it. Cut the flowers to the required lengths and bind them in clusters using a stubb wire. When you have made half a dozen, place them onto the backing to determine their direction and density. Unravel some wire, bringing it underneath the backing; place the first bunch on the backing, wire it tightly in position (fig 1). Continue in this way and do not cut the wire, you will need it for all the subsequent bunches; keep winding the wire round, lifting the swag gently. At this stage incorporate some ribbons or bows if you wish; tie or wire them onto the backing, making the bow first, using a stubb wire. Make sure they sit quite flat on the swag and look as natural as possible with the flowers (fig 2). You can also make pendants to go with the swag; they are quite attractive hanging down from each side. Use

the same method as when making the swag, but hang the loop on the end hooks to create a trailing effect.

The choice of dried flowers for seasonal swags should mirror the colours in the natural world.

Spring swag
In Spring, work with yellows, creams and greens. Aim to create a swag which is an indoor reflection of growth, new life and the fresh colours which are now apparent outside. In the garden the dominant colours are fresh and new: yellow daffodils, brightly coloured tulips and crocuses and the pale green of emergent leaves. For your choice of dried flowers use little pieces of lonas, tansy or achillea heads, which can be taken apart and smaller sections used; yellow helichrysums, sea lavender or caspia to back the clusters; pale green oats or phalaris, gypsophila, achillea 'pearl', leaves or tiny pieces of fern. Bind this combination together on some dark green or gold silk dressing-gown-type cord, and you

will have a swag that can also be used at Easter.

Summer swag

Summer is a time of floral variety, bright colours and warm sunny days. Think, therefore, in terms of warm colours: deep pinks, reds, creams, orange – great mixes of colour to resemble flower borders. You will have to dry plant material early on in the summer, although shops that supply dried flowers usually have stocks of summer flowers right through the year. Rose buds, lavender, gypsophila, deep pink helichrysum, larkspurs in dusty pinks and faded lilacs, pale green corn and alchemilla all mix well together. If you are growing helichrysum or lavender in your garden, place them in the swag to dry naturally, the lavender will fill the room with a beautiful fragrance. Attach wide, pale pink satin ribbons to the swag and use a light-coloured soft rope for the backing and the end result should be a swag full of charm and variety. Place it over a doorway, run it up the banister, or simply on a wall, hanging from two picture hooks – an attractive alternative to other wall decorations.

Herbs grow in abundance during the summer months: try weaving fresh herbs onto a length of plaited raffia to hang on the kitchen wall. The swag is usually raided by the cook, so it will not be a permanent fixture; but it will be a fragrant and attractive addition to the kitchen for a few months, at least.

Autumn swag

Autumn is the best time to make a swag, as the full choice of the summer's flowers is at your disposal. Again, your choice of colours should match the natural hues of this mellow, fruitful time of year. Oranges, russets and ochres are favourites, so choose pieces of morrison, deep helichrysum, achillea, carthamus buds, cream broom bloom, leaves and shimmering oats, to achieve the desired effect. Alternatively, try mixing dark-brown grasses with orange flowers, white larkspur, nigella pods, poppy heads and acroclinium daisies. Try to have a preconceived idea of the shape you wish to create and then choose the flowers accordingly. A swag made totally of greenery – leaves, grasses and ferns – creates a suitable autumnal feel. The addition of beech nuts or dried chestnut cases enhances the seasonal effect.

Winter swag

Winter means short, gloomy days quickly turning to long nights. Fog, snow and ice outside, warm log fires inside. Make a swag to mirror the warm glow of the burning embers. So choose bright-red rose buds, peony heads, rhodanthe daisies, hydrangea florets; or blue delphinium, xeranthemum, lavender, sea holly with deep wine colours such as amaranthus or kangaroo paw. Work to a red theme, using red bottle brush, dyed red broom bloom, phalaris or lagurus. Mix with pink rhodanthe, pieces of green hydrangea and a touch of achillea 'pearl'. Back this onto a rope or scarlet cord and add tartan ribbons to enhance the colour scheme. Such a combination of glowing colours will bring warmth to any home at winter time.

CHAPTER 6
INTERIOR DESIGN WITH A FLORAL THEME

In the preceding chapters, I looked at the principal dried flower types, their shapes and sizes, popular containers and how to make basic arrangements. In this chapter I shall combine all this knowledge and take it one step further. Provided that great care has been taken over the choice of colour and overall shape of the arrangement, dried flower displays can integrate beautifully with the decor of a room. Floral arrangements are an important aspect of thematic interior design.

Due consideration should be given to the colours of curtains, loose-covers and paintwork when choosing the flowers – a good florist will always offer assistance. The style of the room dictates the style of the arrangement. The choice of container is also important – a rustic display in a terracotta pot would look out of place in a chic sitting-room. A neutral arrangement of creams and greens will complement most colour schemes. Although the aim is to achieve harmony, you do not want the arrangement to get 'lost' in a room: one contrasting colour usually allows the arrangement to be seen.

I have put together ten dried flower arrangements, together with a suitable container, and suggested a room where each might be appropriately positioned.

BLUE AND WHITE: GUEST BEDROOM

Blue and white is a popular colour combination; its inherent 'freshness' makes it an ideal display for kitchens. The photograph, however, is of a guest bedroom. I have included a splash of pink statice to pick out the pink in the wash bowl and jug. The blue and white flowers contrast with the curtain fabric, walls and bed coverings. Being a guest room, it is very useful to have a display to hand should someone arrive at a moment's notice. These flowers are tucked into the corner, out of the way of bright sunlight and should serve the room for several years.

The flowers
Blue larkspur, monkshood, lavender, pink statice, sea holly, lilac statice, oats, phalaris, white acroclinium daisies, gypsophila and adiantum fern.

The container
A jug in a wash bowl – this arrangement is very informal. Put the flowers in the jug in great clusters to give an easy country look; the shape of the jug lends itself to height and the flowers will bend naturally into the curves. No plastic foam is necessary as the height of the jug gives sufficient support.

How to make it
Take the longest flowers first and place them in the vase to form a triangular shape: allow the flowers to fall to the lip of the jug. The handle will balance the shape formed by the lip. Put the rest of the flowers in the jug in small bunches, adding the grasses last of all to correct the shape and fill any unsightly gaps. Adjust the height accordingly. Put the 'pointed' flowers in the centre of the display if it is to be seen from all sides. Clay in the bottom of the container will provide the support.

CREAMS, GREENS, REDS AND PINKS: ENTRANCE HALL

The emphasis is on whites and creams in this entrance hall. Without these light shades the whole effect would have been lost, so luscious is the wall covering.

The basket on the hall table is not so large that the flow of traffic will be impeded; other objects may be placed on the table without disturbing its purpose. There is no sunlight to fade the radiant colours, and the different textures look most effective against the plain green cloth.

The flowers
Achillea 'pearl', oats, ambrociana, cockscomb, pink and red roses, blue echinops, monkshood.

The container
A white, lacquered basket using clay as a base.

How to make it
Place a clip in the bottom of the basket. When the glue has dried, attach the clay or plastic foam and start cutting the flowers to the length you require. This basket will be seen from three sides, so an all-round approach will be best. Taking the longest central flowers first, mark the area with a stem to take note of maximum height required. Start to build up the display by placing flowers around the edge. Gradually increase the height of the flowers as each circle is completed – eventually you meet in the middle. A final touch of achillea 'pearl' will add softness and complete the shape of the display.

Opposite
Pretty Victorian china jug and wash bowl filled with a wonderful display of contrasting shapes and colours. This informal arrangement shows monkshood, statices in pinks and lilacs, oats, quaking grass, white acroclinium daisies, larkspur, adiantum, lipidium, gypsophila, sea holly and phalaris.

ENTRANCE HALL

Opposite and above
White-stained, woven rattan basket filled with a luxurious array of colour. Pink and red roses, cockscomb, echinops, nigella flowers, achillea 'pearl', oats, caspia, sea lavender and ambrociana, all complementing the background wall coverings.

STUDIO LIVING-ROOM

VIBRANT PINKS, REDS AND LILACS:
STUDIO LIVING-ROOM

This is a most eye-catching combination of flowers in an unusual room: red lacquered walls, a marble fireplace, bright pink furnishings and a lilac table. To create a successful floral display would seem an impossible task – but the eventual result is impressive. One has to be outrageous because this arrangement has to be seen from all sides.

The flowers
Red bonnie, pink *Briza segromi*, pink peonies, pink roses, lilac larkspur and pink poker.

The container
Black-stained rattan basket with a clay base.

How to make it
Glue a clip to the middle of the basket. Attach the clay or plastic foam and push down. Begin by making a centre point using the larkspur and pink pokers. Take the bunches of flowers, one at a time, and wire the more fragile flowers together. Red bonnie often benefits from being wired, particularly if the stems have become floppy. After establishing the central point, place four stems into the clay to form a square using slightly shorter lengths than the central one; now add four more stems placed in the gaps below the first four. You should now have some sort of shape to work with. Fill in the edge, then the sections between these marker stems, turning the basket continually to ensure that the balance is correct. Place the briza in last of all, to create a soft and undulating effect.

Opposite and above
Frothy pink display using masses of red bonnie, *Briza segromi*, lilac larkspur, pink poker and peonies, arranged *en masse* in a round, black-stained rattan basket.

LIVING-ROOM

PEACH, APRICOT AND CREAM: LIVING-ROOM

Peach and apricot are the most popular colours used in interior design. This room, with a hint of the Orient, is extreme in its simplicity. Many themes would work, but the simple and uncomplicated display is the most complimentary.

The leaves give shape to the arrangement, quite naturally lending themselves to the gentle curves of the vase. The light, dusky-coloured peonies add warmth, whilst the pampas creates a gentle flowing movement.

The flowers
Bleached eucalyptus, pampas grass and peonies.

The container
Frosted-glass vase filled with pot-pourri to act as a base and to hide the stalks.

How to make it
First, fill the vase with pot-pourri. Position the leaves, they will be anchored naturally by the pot-pourri and are easily moved around should you wish to alter the angle of the display. Cut the peonies to the length required and use these to fill the spaces between the leaves. Finally, add the pampas grass to create the sensation of gentle movement within the arrangement. Let the stems bend slightly at an angle so that the fronds fall naturally. The pampas must look attractive from all sides of the display.

Opposite and above
Stunningly simple peaches
and cream decoration using
pampas grass, bleached
eucalyptus leaves and pale
pink peonies. Crisp lines
contrast with the softly falling
flowers in the table display.

CORRIDOR

BLACK, ORANGE, GREEN AND CREAM: CORRIDOR

One has to treat highly patterned vases with great respect, since they can overpower the flowers and the arrangement will look a mess. If you have chosen a patterned container place it in simple, stark surroundings where it will be noticed. In a corridor, the material should always be as robust as possible.

The flowers
Green eucalyptus, morrison, centaurea, carthamus, blue brunia and kangaroo paw.

The container
Large white ceramic vase with green, black, orange, blue and yellow patterned design.

How to make it
Place a large lump of clay in the bottom of the vase – it will be supporting a number of heavy eucalyptus branches. The eucalyptus branches give the basic shape. Add the other flowers one type at a time: kangaroo paw, followed by the morrison, centaurea, carthamus and finally the bobbly blue brunia.

Brightly coloured ceramic vase in a stylishly stark setting. A mixture of eucalyptus, morrison, centaurea, bright blue brunia, kangaroo paw and carthamus combine to make the perfect decoration.

LIVING-ROOM

PINK CHINTZ LIVING-ROOM

Chintzes are extremely popular in England; it is an easy style which makes you feel at home and comfortable. The attractive muted shades of dried flowers harmonize perfectly with chintz patterns. The white walls in this room add definition to the decor and the informal, but stylish display and container, complete the scene.

The flowers
Pink larkspur, pink helichrysum, lilac statice, green eucalyptus, white larkspur, white *Helichrysum vestium*, pink rhodanthe, poppy heads, grey brunia, pink baby star, gomphrena, gypsophila, caspia and pink roses.

The container
Fruit-gathering vine basket.

How to make it
Place two clips in the bottom of the basket, equal distances apart. Attach plastic foam or some clay to each of them, so that the flower stems will not have to stretch across the length of the basket. Start by forming the shape with the larkspur and caspia, reserve a little caspia for finishing off, should the arrangement become too flat. Use the other flowers, making clusters with the daisies; wire the helichrysum and the roses if necessary, and place them in towards the end. Finish with the gypsophila, forming a cloudy haze that will give the basket a muted, misty look, thus matching the surrounding fabric.

Opposite and above
A glorious array of muted
chintz colours in pinks,
creams, greens and greys
designed to match the curtain
and chair fabric. The vine
country basket is filled with
caspia, silver brunia, statice,
pink rhodanthe daisies,
helichrysum, poppy heads,
white *Helichrysum vestium*,
gomphrena, eucalyptus
leaves, pink baby star and
gypsophila.

DINING-ROOM

EXOTICA

Africa and Australia can boast the most
extraordinary indigenous plants and flowers,
of many weird and wonderful shapes and
sizes. They mix well together, creating an
individual look which is perfect in a rustic
setting. These exotic displays look most
impressive in rather unusual surroundings.
This formal lunch table is in a very stark room
in a farmhouse; dark elegant furniture
contrasts well with the rough weave of the
basket, and the formality of the table setting.

The flowers
Banksias, proteas, dryandras, eucalyptus,
teasles, lilac kangaroo paw, cup leaf hakea and
curly grass.

The container
Rough-weave vine basket.

How to make it
Place a clip in the bottom of the basket and
attach the clay or plastic foam. Cut the
eucalyptus stems to the lengths you require
and use them to form a circle round the edge of
the container, so that the leaves tumble prettily
over the sides. Cut all the proteas and banksias
to length and place them in symmetrically, add
all the other varieties and keep filling in the
different spaces. Finally, make the wispy
shapes with the curly grass.

Opposite and above
Proteas, banksias, curly grass, eucalyptus, teasles and hakea leaf in an appropriately rustic basket. This exotic yet rather rustic arrangement contrasts with the formality of the dining table. The display is low enough not to be a nuisance but sufficiently striking to make an impact.

Pastel-glazed cotton fabric with
a blue trim.

BLUE, APRICOT, GREEN AND WHITE: MASTER BEDROOM

In large rooms such as this, a floor display will not be in the way and can be an excellent alternative to a piece of furniture. This arrangement is just under the window ledge, therefore avoiding the worst of the sun's rays. However, make the display so that it is attractive from all sides, so that it can be turned should any bleaching occur.

The flowers
Densi-flora, pink larkspur, white larkspur, pink roses, blue glixia, sea holly, achillea 'pearl', oats, blue hydrangeas and pink peonies.

The container
Rope flower basket and plastic foam base – clay often attracts damp on the floor and the flowers will develop mildew.

How to make it
Place a clip on the bottom of the basket and attach a large block of plastic foam. Put the pointed flowers in first having previously cut them to size. Form the shape with these, then follow with clusters of the other flowers. Always work systematically through the flower types. Finish off with the achillea 'pearl'. Use only small amounts of blue glixia as, in quantity, it will overpower the arrangement.

MASTER BEDROOM

Picturesque rope floor-basket placed just under the sun's path. The arrangement consists of grasses, peonies, blue ti-tree, sea holly, a dash of vivid blue glixia, white statice, peach statice, blue hydrangea, roses and Australian densiflors.

FARMHOUSE KITCHEN

Left and overleaf
An interesting selection of
pastel garden flowers for a
farmhouse kitchen. Roses,
peonies, lavender, alchemilla,
sea holly, gypsophila, deep
blue delphinium and wisps of
caspia.

PASTELS: FARMHOUSE KITCHEN

This kitchen is white walled, with blue and white accessories, such as all the visible crockery. Huge baskets of dried flowers sit on high beams. The wood in the kitchen is predominently pine: this overall rustic look lends itself to natural garden flowers. Pinks, lavenders, deep powder blues, yellow-greens, and creams blend beautifully with these surroundings. The arrangement is not so large that it intrudes on the general busy hubbub of the kitchen, and it is easily portable should it get in the way. The display, which is attractive from all sides, is a perfect emergency table centre for the dinning-room since the flowers are low, the basket hazy and unobtrusive.

The flowers
Lavender, sea holly, lilac larkspur, pink roses, pink peonies, alchemilla, fine gypsophila, blue and pale lilac hydrangeas, caspia and white statice.

The container
A narrow-weave wicker basket with handle over. A clay base is used.

How to make it
Place a clip in the bottom and attach the clay or plastic foam to the clip. Place all the flowers in the basket, having formed mini bunches of each – about the size of the hydrangea heads. Work round the basket in a circle, in a very informal way, developing the shape as you go. This arrangement is quick and simple to make.

SALMON AND WHITE: HOTEL DINING-ROOM

Dried flowers, which are both robust and virtually everlasting, are an appropriate decoration in a hotel dining-room. Here are two ideas, both conceived with the utmost simplicity: a frosted glass jar containing several stems of pure white honesty; and a small, crisp white ceramic vase, displaying eucalyptus dyed salmon pink to match the wallpaper. Both are attractive, uncluttered and catch the light magnificently in their window position.

The flowers
1) Honesty.
2) Dyed eucalyptus.

The containers
1) Frosted glass container, with a small amount of clay to support the stems.
2) White modern ceramic vase with a small amount of clay.

How to make them
These are incredibly simple arrangements to make. Place a very small amount of clay in the bottom of both containers. Press down hard in the glass one, so that it will not be illuminated by the light. Take small stems cut to size and place these in the vase at different angles until you are pleased with the shape they form.

Simple displays are often the most striking and the light in this room shows them off to perfection. Honesty and eucalyptus are both appropriately sturdy for constant use.

CHAPTER 7
WEDDING DISPLAYS

Flowers are one of the most important accessories at a wedding. Great care, attention to detail and no small amount of imagination go into the preparation of wedding displays. The colours and style of the flowers are usually chosen by the bride, to enhance and complement her dress and those of the bridesmaids. Preserving fresh flowers is a very difficult and time-consuming process, since the displays have to be taken apart and each flower dried in the appropriate way. This must be done the moment the wedding is over, by someone who is skilled in the art.

Today, many people are choosing artifical or dried flowers for weddings so that everyone concerned may have a family keepsake. Dried flowers are an original and versatile alternative to fresh flowers. They can be prepared weeks in advance of the wedding day, thus allowing for alterations to the colour and style of the arrangement.

Dried flowers can be used to make all the traditional trappings: the bride's bouquet and head-dress; the bridesmaids' baskets; hoops; table displays and place settings; and in the church, pew ends, swags and pedestal displays. The displays can be formal or informal, depending on the style of wedding and the character and setting of the church.

These wedding accessories are made from a mixture of pink larkspur, oats, adiantum, caspia, phalaris, pink glixia, pink baby star, achillea 'pearl', gypsophila and cream satin ribbons. In the foreground: the swag, and a small bridesmaid's basket. On the left: the bride's bouquet. Top centre: the head-dress. On the right: bridesmaid's hoop and basket (the basket can also be used for a table display).

Left
An informal bride's bouquet
tied with satin ribbon.
Right
Bridesmaid's basket, ribbons
bind the handle.

THE BRIDE'S ACCESSORIES

BOUQUET

Materials required
1 The flowers.
2 Stubb wire and rose wire, tape.
3 Strong scissors.
4 Ribbons.

The bouquet in the photograph is made by arranging flowers in groups and layers. Find a table where you will have plenty of room to manoeuvre, and where you can leave all your materials uninterrupted until you have finished the job.

Place the longest fern-type flowers onto the table, then using each of the flowers in turn, form the overall shape of the arrangement. Arrange the flowers in ever-decreasing lengths towards the middle of the bouquet, this will create a full effect on the top. Wire in any flowers that may have broken or are too short; conceal these among the other flower stems so that they will not show at the end.

When you have completed this stage, pick the bouquet up carefully and, holding it tightly, place any remaining single stems into obvious gaps or where there is an imbalance of flowers. Then, with the other hand, wire or tape the stems tightly in position before attaching the ribbons. The ribbons could take the form of a single, floppy bow at the front of the bouquet, or layers of ribbon wound over the stems to form a handle. Start by winding tightly, from the stems at the base towards the flowers, finishing with a bow and trailing ribbon ends – this creates an air of formality.

THE HEAD-DRESS

Both the bride and the bridesmaids can wear head-dresses. You can buy the frame at wedding accessory or haberdashery shops. These normally take the form of lengths of soft wire which can be cut to the required size. Make provision for a couple of hooks at the ends, by bending the wire about half an inch on each side; these join together at the back of the head-dress.

Materials required
1 The wire frame.
2 Plenty of narrow satin ribbon to cover the frame, at least three times its length, and a wider piece for the bow at the back – allow for tails.
3 A reel of fine rose wire and fine stubb wire (tape is also useful).
4 Strong florist's scissors.
5 Glue, tape or a needle and thread.
6 The flowers.

Bend the frame to the shape you require, then bind the ribbon around the frame; attach the first piece with tape, glue or by sewing it tightly together. You will finish off in exactly the same way at the other end. Follow the same guidelines that apply to making swags: form little clusters of flowers and wire them onto the frame using the reel of fine rose wire, or light-coloured tape. The flowers should be quite full so that no wires will be visible when the head-dress is in place. Attach a bow to the back hook and allow a trail of ribbon to fall in a cascade.

BASKETS

The bride and bridesmaids might choose to carry little baskets as an alternative to bouquets and posies. These are generically known as bridesmaid's baskets and are filled with flowers and finished off with trailing ribbon. Make these baskets in the same way as described in Chapter 3.

Materials required
1 The baskets.
2 The flowers.
3 Plastic foam (Oasis) (clay is too heavy to carry down the aisle).
4 Strong scissors.
5 Some wires for mending or supporting the flowers.
6 Ribbons to bind round the handle, and a wider ribbon for the bow and trail.

The arrangement should look full and fluffy and very feminine, with ribbons criss-crossing the handle. Attach bows to each side of the base of the handle, adding long, single trailing pieces if desired. The size of the baskets should be in proportion to the size of the children who will carry them.

The hoop is made from a hula-hoop tightly ribboned and decorated with flowers. A cluster of ribbons is attached at one end to hang prettily when it is being carried.

HOOPS

Hoops are a charming, old-fashioned idea which are traditionally made of wood – original wooden hoops are very rare. I have improvized with a plastic hoola-hoop covered with yards of satin ribbon encased with flowers.

Materials required
1 Hoop made of wood or plastic.
2 Ten metres of cream satin ribbon.
3 Glue, tape or needle and thread.
4 Stubb wires.
5 Strong scissors.
6 The flowers.

If you are using a plastic hula-hoop, try to buy a small one. If you buy a large one, pull the join apart and cut off any excess length. Remember, children usually carry these at weddings, so make sure the size will be in proportion to the size of the child.

Cover the hoop with the ribbon, winding it round and round, each piece just overlapping the last. Sew, glue or tape the first piece and the last piece and use a large ribbon to cover the join. Begin by placing the clusters of flowers in the same way as described for making the swag in Chapter 5. Work from the back outwards; do not use more wire than is absolutely necessary because the wire may be visible when the hoop is being carried.

114

An ancient church with carved pew ends adorned with a delightful swag and pew end garland. The displays are kept in place with satin ribbon.

THE CHURCH

Small country churches with old-fashioned carved pew ends can look lovely when filled with flowers. Modern churches will look equally charming if the display is sympathetic to a change in atmosphere and style. Registry offices can also be decorated by placing a pew end of dried flowers on the backs of the chairs or at the end of the seats.

Materials required

1 A plastic foam or round (Oasis).
2 Stubb wires.
3 A reel of wire.
4 The flowers.
5 Strong scissors.
6 Ribbons to match.

Take the plastic foam and make sure there is a side that will sit flat against the pew. Cut the

ball in half, or slice a wedge off one side to make it lie flat; place the flat side down and prepare the flowers. Form the shape by using the spiky ones first, such as larkspur, fern and oats. Place the outside-edge flowers in the display and, taking account of the shape you wish to create, choose your flowers and work towards the middle. The shape in the photograph is an oval. The flowers, placed in almost symmetrically, create a certain 'fullness'. The ribbon is wired into the plastic foam to give it support and is attached to the top, bottom and centre of the display. A large loop enables the top to hang over the pew end. Wire the two ends of the loop together and attach a strong, long stubb wire, which is then pushed through the plastic foam back, curving the end when it protrudes. Pull it back slightly to catch onto the end thus giving support to the ribbon. The ribbon should be at a level just above the plastic foam block and invisible behind the flowers. Tie a big floppy bow and wire it into the back at the bottom of the display, this will hang down naturally against the wood.

It is always advisable to measure how much loop you will need to hang the display from the pew end; they vary enormously from church to church. Ensure that the arrangements are firmly attached to the pew ends, as many will be jostled by guests as they enter and leave the church.

SWAGS

Swags have two purposes at a wedding: the first is to decorate the church, effectively joining the pews; and the second is to adorn the sides of long, hanging table-cloths at the reception. Again, the distance between the pews and the length of the tables will equate with the measurements of the swags. In the church, there are several ways to hang swags: from a pew end looping down to join the middle of the display; or from the tops of the pew ends, meeting the next pew end in line. Remember one part of the swag must be fixed before the ceremony; the usher can join the other end to close the pews after the guests are seated.

Swags for the table sides should be fixed on firmly with safety pins or, if they are particularly heavy, they can be sewn onto the back of the cloth.

Materials required
1 Length of silk cord, preferably white, cream, pale pink or green.
2 Strong scissors.
3 Stubb wires and a reel of wire.
4 Cream double-sided satin ribbon.
5 The flowers.

The swag is made in exactly the same way as described in Chapter 5, except you would add extra ribbon at each end in order to hang it successfully from the pews.

FLORAL ARRANGEMENTS

It is advisable to discuss the general style of the floral arrangements in the church with the clergyman. Churches usually have their own accessories and containers and this might influence your choice of arrangement. Generally, church displays are large-format and triangular in shape. Church displays can be made in the same way as vase arrangements described in Chapter 3, though trailing, pedestal displays are very popular at weddings.

THE RECEPTION

The principal tables should be decorated with long, trailing central displays; while small baskets or vases look fine on side tables. If there are not too many guests, you might like to make tiny bouquet place settings, which could then be kept by the guests as mementoes. These tiny bouquets are made up like clusters for swags, and finished off with a small piece of ribbon. A display in a silver chalice could be made for the top of the cake – do not make this too large or overpowering.

If the reception is being held in a marquee, garlands on the central poles, with a mass of trailing ribbons falling almost to the ground, are very effective. Alternatively pin small clusters of flowers to ribbon wound round the poles. Complete the scene with swags adorning the top table.

Opposite
The flowers for this pew end perfectly match the other wedding accessories in pale pinks, cream and greens. Satin ribbons are used to loop the flowers over the pew, and to trail from a bow attached to the base.

CHAPTER 8

FESTIVE FLORAL ARRANGEMENTS

An array of traditional Christmas colours: beautifully decorated garland, made with fresh pine, red roses, red glixia, red anaphalis, cream helichrysum, sparkly flax, gypsophila, sea lavender and cones. Tartan bows give a festive air to the ring. Top right: Small straw garland made with tilancia, *Bromus formus*, red roses, sea lavender and nigella pods bound with deep-green velvet ribbons. Bottom right: Deep-brown, thick wicker garland made simply with three main clusters of fresh pine, green hydrangea, red roses, cream helichrysum and tiny silver baubles, bound with a large, green velvet ribbon bow. Bottom left: Rustic basket crammed full of bright scarlet broom bloom. Middle left: Flat-backed rustic basket of trailing fresh pine. Additional material includes red roses, green hydrangea, cones and tartan ribbons.

Traditionally, Christmas is a time for making decorations in the home, bringing in evergreens, hanging cards and decorating the tree. Dried flowers are a pleasant and original alternative to combine with green foliage or to make a Christmas arrangement that does not necessarily have to reflect the traditional red, white and green – one can blend all sorts of winter colours together to make a festive display. An all-white flower basket with a hint of silver or gold can create a luminous effect. A combination of olive green, yellow ochre, and a dullish red with green or gold ribbons or bobbles looks attractive and different. You can make extraordinary swags and garlands to blend with your theme, be it traditional or avant guard. Try to work with a limited choice of colour: one or two shades mixed with evergreens create surprisingly effective displays. Other ideas for Christmas include colourful place settings and a Christmas tree created out of dried flowers.

CHRISTMAS TREES

One associates Christmas trees with deep-green, luscious-smelling pine. Try experimenting with a dried flower Christmas tree, possibly for a side table. Plastic foam cones can be purchased at most florists or garden centres. Cover the exterior with wire netting (this will reinforce the plastic foam and make it less likely to disintegrate) and encase the cone with moss. Place your decorations into the base, starting with the rather more bulky foliage, and sea lavender or hydrangea. Continue with cones, nuts, baubles – in fact, anything which is suitable for a festive decoration.

Experiment by making a tree made entirely from deep-green ruscus and red berries (which can be bought at florists). Refer to Chapter 5 before making the base.

One does not necessarily have to keep to a cone shape, a round pom-pom tree will be equally as effective. A very pretty way to make one is by spraying hydrangea heads in silver or gold and then covering them with a light film of spray glue. Place the heads in a paper bag filled with glitter and shake until the glue has been coated with the glitter – then stick the flowers into the tree. The sparkling effect created by the judicious use of lighting is worth all the effort.

In order to make a large Christmas tree (like the one shown in the photograph) you will need a large number of plastic foam blocks and very strong adhesive, a stave for the central support, and a very sharp craft knife to cut it to a conical shape.

Place the pole into a pot and set in plaster of Paris. Stick the blocks together and then cut them to form a round. Make the bottom layer first, then using less blocks and moulding as the shape is formed, build up the tree to the size you wish. Having impaled the largest round on the plastic foam, glue this one to successive pieces until the shape is complete and firmly secured. Cover the 'framework' with wire netting as described in Chapter 5 and then start the floral decoration. If you wish to emulate the tree shown in the photograph you will need plenty of the following types of plants: sea lavender; preserved foliage; *Helichrysum vestium*; ammobium daisies; white sago; white statice; caspia; large fir-cones; green velvet ribbon; and a set of fairy lights. In addition you will need decorations of your choice and three sets of tree beads.

Use the sea lavender and foliage first and then arrange the fairy lights. Systematically work through the flowers followed by the cones, decorations and finally the ribbons.

A Christmas tree made from dried flowers will last for years if it is given the correct care and attention. When Christmas is over wrap it in dark tissue paper and place it in a dark, dry cupboard.

This dried flower Christmas tree in original whites and browns is decorated with silver and clear glass baubles and beads. To make the tree use sea lavender as a base and add crisp white statice, *Helichrysum vestium*, ammobium daisies, sago flower, oak, beech and pittosporum leaves, small and large cones, deep green velvet ribbons and clear fairy lights. Place the end result in a round wicker basket having initially put the tree in a large plastic flowerpot.

The Christmas tree in position in the candlelit room.

Close detail of red, white and green garland.

Inset
Cover a wire frame with moss and attach festive flowers and foliage to make a traditional Christmas garland.

GARLANDS

Traditionally, garlands adorn exterior doors. Dried flower garlands, however, are interior Christmas displays. They look splendid hanging from doors, beams, archways or mantlepieces – perhaps with a gracious swag beneath. There are various ready-made wicker rings on the market, but you can make a wire ring and cover it with moss before smothering it with festive flowers and a few contrasting untreated evergreens. Vivid 'reds' can be found in flowers such as helichrysum, bottle brush, celosia (cockscomb), red roses, dyed phalaris, lagurus and anaphalis; while beech leaves, ruscus, green amaranthus, grasses and Australian hollyoak make a pleasing change from more traditional evergreens. Creams and whites are always available in the form of white *Helichrysum vestium*, cream broom bloom, achillea 'pearl', gypsophila, ammobium daisies and white statice. Many plants are excellent candidates for spraying with gold or silver paints: fir-cones, seed pods, honesty, Chinese lanterns and nigella pods are but a few examples.

SWAGS

Swags make lovely decorations in any home, hung on the mantlepiece or suspended across the banisters or balustrade. It is a time-consuming process, but if you decide to mix conifers and evergreens with the dried flowers, the bulky greenery will soon build up and the swag will quickly be completed. The basic methods for making swags were discussed in Chapter 5: Christmas swags vary only in the choice of material. A festive colour theme combined with seasonal plants and accessories is very effective. The Christmas swag seen in

the photograph is made from all-white flowers, with a touch of adianthum fern, fir-cones and green velvet ribbon. The backing of white silk cord can be purchased from haberdashery shops. With the exception of the bulky preserved leaves, the material used is the same as was used to make the Christmas tree.

Clusters of pine, roses, ruscus, a touch of sea lavender and some grass, wired to a moss-covered wire frame make an attractive swag, particularly if the chain is broken at intervals with ribbons. If the swag is made entirely from dried flowers, it can be wrapped in dark tissue paper and stored until next year.

Matching swag in creams and browns graciously decorates the balustrade.

PLACE SETTINGS

Place settings can be made in little baskets, which sit unobtrusively by the table-mats or cutlery. Alternatively, little bouquets, the size of button holes, can be laid on the table napkins. Trim the bouquets with ribbons and the guests can keep them as a memento of the evening.

PRESENTS

Home-made gifts are always appreciated and dried flowers give ample scope for the practical pair of hands. Lavender collected in the summer can be made into pretty lavender bags and tied with trailing ribbons. Markets and remnant shops are good sources of squares of old-fashioned lace or organza.

Swags, garlands, trees and little bouquets of flowers all make beautiful presents. Pressed-flower pictures are particularly popular – collect the flowers throughout the year to ensure plenty of choice near to Christmas. Go

collecting on a day when the flowers are moisture free, never when it is raining or after a heavy dew. Place the flowers between blotting paper and put them under a heavy weight for six weeks. Do not try to look at them before the six weeks have passed.

To make pictures, you will need glue, backing paper, tweezers, scissors and lots of patience! Arrange the flowers on the backing paper according to a preplanned design and stick them down with a small amount of glue. The picture should be framed and made airtight: the flowers will go mouldy if exposed to the damp air. Avoid direct sunlight because the picture will fade quickly.

Pot-pourri has become enormously popular over the past few years – the choice of fragance and texture is quite mind-boggling. A simple, but pretty idea for a present is to wire flower heads to the handle and outside edge of a basket, in the same way as you would for a swag or garland, and fill the cavity with pot-pourri of your choice. As always, bows and ribbons complete the effect.

Candle ring and tiny place setting baskets in whites and browns complete the Christmas table setting.

Opposite
Swag, candle ring and place setting baskets. Note the flower heads have been placed very prominently 'face upwards' to give a shimmering effect in the candlelit atmosphere.

Medium-sized plastic foam sphere crammed full of sea lavender, eucalyptus, caspia, red roses, cockscomb, ambrociana, cream helichrysum, fir-cones and narrow, green-velvet ribbons.

126

POM-POMS

Pom-poms made from plastic foam balls, both large and small, are original and extremely attractive Christmas decorations. Many choose to hang them over tables in preference to the traditional vase. Their basic construction is exactly the same as for pom-pom trees, but before starting to decorate the ball, insert a long, sturdy stubb wire through the middle. Bend it in two so that it forms a loop (fig 1) from which it will hang. It helps to thread a coloured ribbon through it before you start, because when the flowers are put in place the wire can get lost amongst the flowers and stems.

Making the pom-pom is much easier if you hang it from a hook above your work surface;

you can form a better 'round' if you can turn it gently during the making process. Cut all the flowers, keeping them to a sensible length: remember the base flowers will be slightly shorter than the second flowers, so allow for this when you are deciding on the finished size. Start by working on a small area to test the length. When you have fully established the size, place the flowers (or basic filler) in north, south, east and west positions and fill in section by section, turning the pom-pom occasionally to test its 'roundness'. Snip off any excess length, especially if you are using sea lavender, and before you place the next flowers in position, snip off any twigs. Complete the pom-pom by attaching dangling ribbons to the base and into the ball itself at regular intervals.

How to make a pom-pom

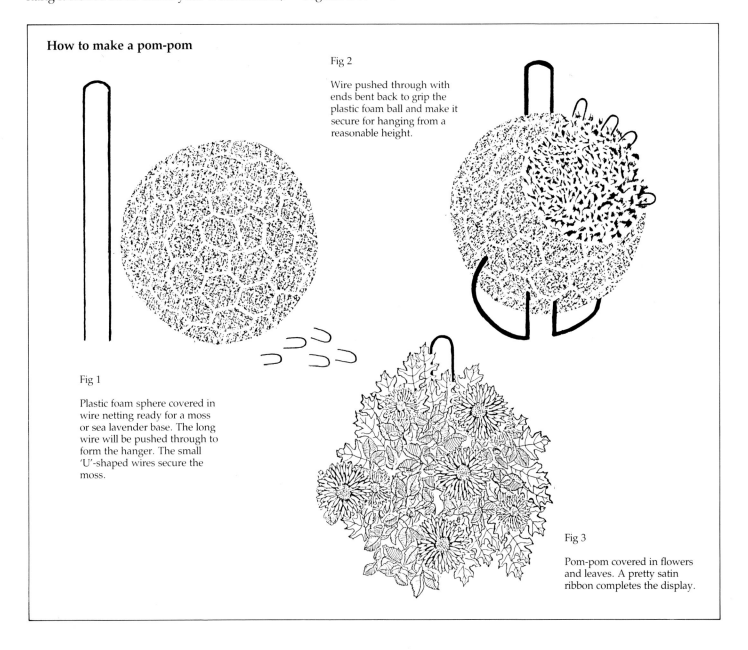

Fig 2

Wire pushed through with ends bent back to grip the plastic foam ball and make it secure for hanging from a reasonable height.

Fig 1

Plastic foam sphere covered in wire netting ready for a moss or sea lavender base. The long wire will be pushed through to form the hanger. The small 'U'-shaped wires secure the moss.

Fig 3

Pom-pom covered in flowers and leaves. A pretty satin ribbon completes the display.

127

CHAPTER 9

OTHER IDEAS

Wheatsheaf with plaited tie.
Rosebud heads wired onto the
plait create a splash of colour.

In this chapter I shall explore the area beyond conventional dried flower displays. Such is the versatility of dried flowers, large, ambitious arrangements do not always have to steal the show.

WHEATSHEAF

A wheatsheaf will either hang from a wall or ceiling or stand on the floor. They are most attractive in kitchens but are equally at home in most parts of the house. They are traditionally made for harvest thanksgiving.

To make a wheatsheaf like the one shown in the photograph you will need the following items:

Materials required

1 Twelve-fourteen large bunches of wheat (six-eight for a smaller sheaf).
2 Strong, long stubb wires or a reel of wire.
3 Florist's scissors and wire cutters.
4 Six roses for the plait (optional).

Place a large sheet of paper on the floor and divide the wheat into bunches of twenty pieces. The heads of the wheat should all be level before the wire is secured. Continue to make up small bunches of wheat until all but twelve strands remain – these are for the plait. Lay all the bunches in rows within easy reach. Take six in your hands and make sure they are all in the same position. Then take bunch by bunch making layer upon layer, working in a circle rather as if one was making a giant posy.

Fresh green-coloured wheatsheaf used as decoration for a guest bedroom.

129

The middle bunches should be higher than the next layer of bunches to create a slightly pointed shape. When you have finished, tie the wheat together with wire from the reel of wire. Plait the remaining twelve strands together and secure these to the back, again with the wire. Cover the plait with six pre-wired roses.

If the sheaf is to stand, make sure you level off the bottom so all the lengths are even, thereby ensuring that it will balance properly. If it is to hang, trim off any unsightly strands and follow the same procedure as for the floor finish. It is wise to ensure that the wire supporting the sheaf, and the hook from which it will hang, are secure.

SMALL VASES AND BASKETS

Small vases and baskets are perfect for gifts and to decorate small corners of your home. They require very few flowers and can be made quite quickly. One can often make a small arrangement from the left overs of larger displays in small containers such as egg cups, ramekins and small coffee cups, as well as tiny vases specially designed for this purpose. Little wooden boxes, cane chests and tiny sweet baskets look delightful when adorned with dried flower arrangements. When making them for presents, wrap them in brightly coloured cellophane paper and finish off with a matching ribbon, preferably one that curls.

From left to right: White pedestal vase, filled with monkshood, achillea 'moonshine', matecaria, caspia and cream helichrysum; blue and white china bowl containing golden achillea, hydrangea, nigella, and gypsophila; pretty blue and white jug filled with sea holly and mini lunaria; little china birds, filled with a selection of oats, achillea 'pearl', gypsophila and mini lunaria; small white pedestal vase full of honesty and mini lunaria.

From left to right: Nest basket filled with oats; small chest containing a selection of ti-tree, densiflora, caspia, sea holly, kangaroo paw, achillea 'moonshine' and achillea 'pearl'; tiny sweet basket with lavender, gypsophila, caspia and acroclinium daisies; bridesmaid's basket filled with sea lavender, nigella, matecaria, adiantum, everlasting daisies and acroclinium daisies; rustic trug filled with sea lavender, oats, mini lunaria, hydrangea and gypsophila.

Rustic pale-green-stained
basket with a huge mass of
phalaris – ideal for a kitchen
display.

BASKETS OF ONE FLOWER TYPE

Single-type flower arrangements make a refreshing change from mixed displays. Despite their inherent simplicity the quest for an eye-catching show can tax one's imagination.

Materials required
1 The basket.
2 A good quantity of clay or a large plastic foam block.
3 Wires for emergency repairs or short stems.
4 The grasses (phalaris).

Place the clay or plastic foam in the basket on the clip, making sure that as much of the bottom of the basket is covered with it as possible. Measure the lengths of the grasses so that they protrude over the rim by about one inch and gradually get longer towards the middle, where they will protrude a maximum of three inches. Begin by building a circular shape; keep turning the basket to ensure that the lengths are even, gradually build up the lengths so that the centre of the display is slightly higher than all the rest. The end result is surprisingly rewarding and under proper lighting the shimmery phalaris looks very effective.

INFORMAL BASKET

Materials required
1 A basket (quite good depth).
2 Clay or plastic foam.
3 Adiantum leaves.
4 Wires for emergency repairs or shorter stems.

Place the clay or plastic foam in the basket on the clip. Take two or three bunches of adiantum, separate the fern-like branches and put them into the clay or plastic foam at different angles. This basket can be made quickly and is really striking when displayed with light seeping through the fronds. The leaves will fade, however, if exposed to direct sunlight.

DOMES

Glass domes were very popular during Victorian times, when not only dried flowers were placed behind the glass but also stuffed animals, birds and fish. These domes, however, have suddenly become popular again and are very much more attractive than they used to be because of the enormous variety of dried flowers now available. Domes are a wonderful solution to the problems associated with placing arrangements in bathrooms, since the steam will not ruin the flowers.

Materials required
1 The glass dome (available in gift, glass and china shops).
2 Plastic foam (Oasis) or clay.
3 Thin wires.
4 Flowers, foliage or a mixture of both.
5 Feather-made butterflies or similar decorations (optional).

Place the clay or plastic foam onto a clip, secured in the centre of the base with glue. Replace the glass and measure the maximum height of the material that will form the display. The flowers should not be too cramped inside the dome or they will spoil and look distorted.

Start your arrangement from the middle, gaining maximum height here. Continue working in a circular motion making sure the floor of the dome is attractively covered before placing the glass over the whole arrangement. This can be the most tricky moment: polish any smears off the inside of the glass, before trying

Thick weave basket filled with
pretty fern-like adiantum
leaves.

Opposite
This glass dome contains
caspia, various grasses,
sterlingia, adiantum fern and
gypsophila. Two butterflies
made from feathers make a
decorative optional extra.

Using three white, starkly modern vases it is an easy exercise to achieve three different, yet equally simple, displays.
Below
The freshness of African everlasting daisies.
Right
A selection of protea and exotica.
Overleaf
Seaweed, conicalgum, bell gum, bell cup grass and jacaranda pods combine to give a curious mixture of shapes and colours.

to cover the base. Squeeze all the material together very gently, then slowly lower the dome, pushing in any little pieces that catch. Give the base a gentle blow before letting the glass down totally to get rid of little pieces of flower debris that may have caught and will prevent the glass from sitting flat. Polish the outside with a duster and place the dome in position.

SAME VASE, DIFFERENT ARRANGEMENT

Using the same container for two or three different arrangements is not only fun, but can

be extremely effective. The container should be plain and versatile. Having chosen very modern vases to illustrate the idea in the photograph it is very important to keep the arrangements ultra simple: either by using one type of flower, grass or leaves; or if you mix flower types, stay with one colour.

Before you begin, experiment with shape, style and height – never cut the stems too short. The most appropriate base for this arrangement is clay or small stones – these will ensure an element of mobility, even when the display is finished. Always handle dried flowers with care, they will snap easily, and take your time – you will be constantly amazed by the fruits of your labour.

CHAPTER 10
IDENTIFICATION

There are hundreds of varieties of flowers and types of foliage which are suitable for drying. The following pages list the most popular in colour co-ordinated spreads. This is not a definitive glossary but the majority of these popular types have been mentioned in this book.

Large bowl containing sea lavender, with limonium caspia shown below.

RED, GREEN AND FOLIAGE

1   Adiantum
2   Oak leaves
3   Leucodendron
4   Daphanoides
5   Witch hazel
6   Eucalyptus round leaf
7   White phylica
8   Vlei-rose
9   Eucalyptus pointed leaf
10 Green broom bloom
11 Cones
12 Basilia
13 Chinese puzzle
14 Ruscus
15 Honesty
16 African grass
17 African grass
18 *Briza segromi*
19 Holly oak
20 Lagurus
21 Cockscomb
22 Glixia
23 Phalaris
24 Broom bloom
25 Anaphalis
26 Bottle brush
27 Red roses
28 Peony
29 Helichrysum
30 Flax (gold sparkly)
31 Beech leaves

BLUE, LILAC AND GREY

1 Middle – Dyed blue brunia
2 Hydrangeas
3 Lilac statice
4 Nigella Bloom
5 Lilac larkspur
6 Nigella pods
7 Amaranthus
8 Xeranthemum
9 Gomphrena
10 Monkswood
11 Pink poker
12 Statice
13 Densiflora
14 Purple larkspur
15 Silver brunia
16 Poppy heads
17 White ti-tree
18 Sea holly
19 Phylica
20 Blue hill flower
21 Echinop
22 Lavender
23 Blue glixia
24 Hydrangeas

EXOTICA

1 Conical gum
2 Recondita
3 Daphanoides
4 Rosettes
5 Cressida
6 *Protea laurifolia*
7 Mini *Protea rogus*
8 *Mimetes hirta*
9 *Banksia occidentalis*
10 Sandplain woody pear
11 Silver brunia
12 Large protea
13 Bell cup stems
14 Bell gum
15 *Repens supurcuts*
16 Leucodendron
17 Dubium
18 Jacaranda pods
19 Kangaroo paw
20 Curly grass
21 Sylfuria bud
22 Purple neriflower
23 *Dryandra obtusa* leaves
24 *Protea compacta*
25 Paranomous
26 Dried seaweed
27 Brachychilton pods
28 Combretia

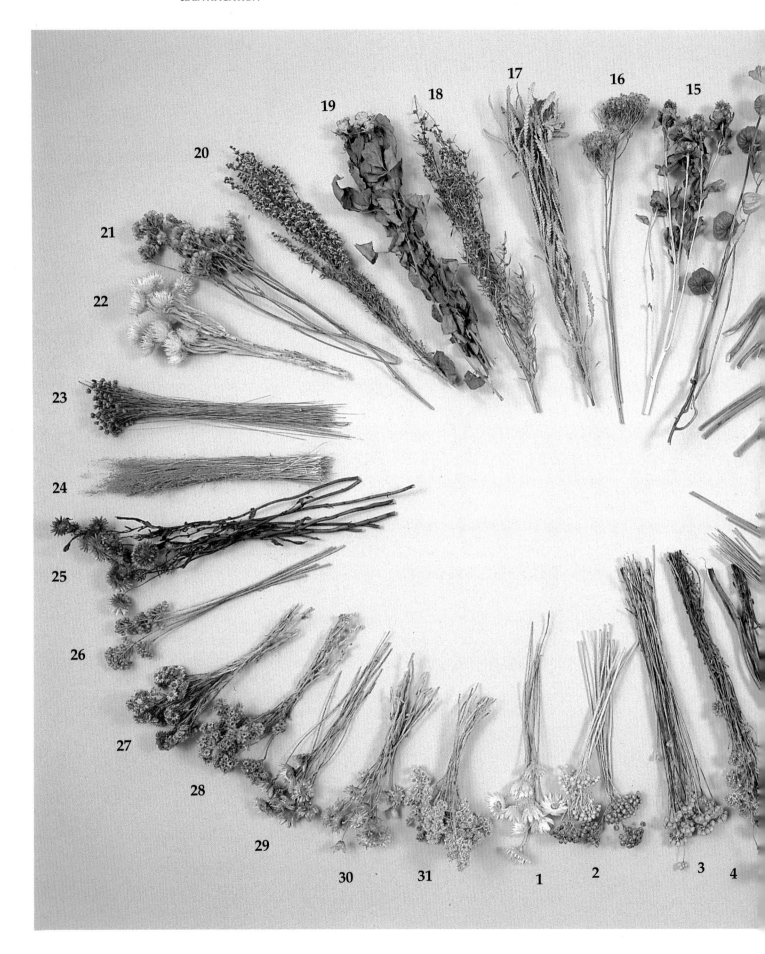

ORANGE, YELLOW, APRICOT AND PEACH

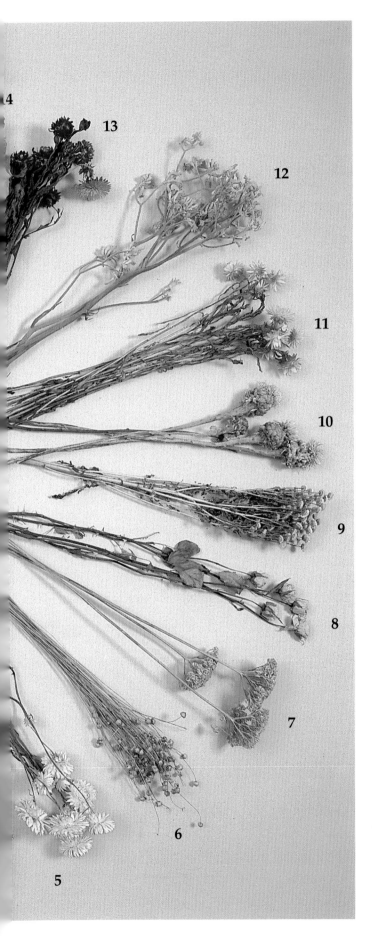

1   Everlasting daisy
2   Hill flowers
3   Lonas
4   Sanfordii
5   Helichrysum (pale yellow)
6   Flax
7   Deep golden achillea
8   Roses
9   Matecaria
10 Centaurea
11 Yellow helichrysum (bright yellow)
12 Kangaroo paw
13 Orange helichrysum
14 Chinese lanterns
15 Carthamus
16 Morrison
17 Dryandra formosa
18 Ti-tree rosa
19 Cream roses
20 Ti-tree
21 Apricot statice
22 Orange-dyed *Helichrysum vestium*
23 Glixia
24 Agrostis
25 Salmon helichrysum
26 Hill flower
27 Sneezy
28 Curry flower
29 Everlasting daisy
30 Top hat daisy
31 Curry flower

PINK

1   *Verticordia brownii*
2   Mountain daisy
3   Ixodia daisy
4   Everlasting daisy
5   Baby star
6   *Helichrysum vestium*
7   Phalaris
8   Red bonnie
9   Gomphrena
10 Larkspur
11 Acroclinium daisy
12 Rose
13 *Briza segromi*
14 Ti-tree
15 Rhodanthe
16 Pink broom bloom
17 Pink poker
18 Helichrysum
19 Mini pink roses
20 Agrostis
21 Pink hill flower
22 Silene
23 Pink peony
24 Curry plant
25 Pink hydrangeas

CREAM AND GREEN

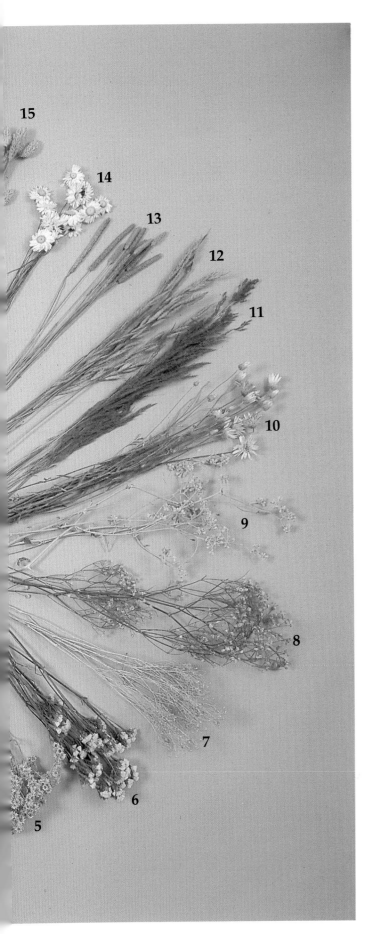

1   Hops
2   Alchemilla
3   Cream peony
4   Chinese puzzle
5   White curry flower
6   White statice
7   Cream broom bloom
8   Gypsophila
9   Sea crest
10 Xeranthemum
11 Festuca
12 *Bromus formus*
13 Phleum
14 Acroclinium daisy
15 Phalaris
16 Oats
17 Polypogon
18 Wheat
19 Pampas grass
20 Mini lunaria
21 Cream larkspur
22 Tiny-headed baby's breath gypsophila
23 Ammobium daisy
24 Cream helichrysum
25 Ti-tree
26 White rhodanthe
27 Achillea 'pearl'
28 Lipidium
29 Ambrociana
30 *Helichrysum vestium*
31 White everlasting daisy
32 Amaranthus
33 Cream hydrangeas
34 Green hydrangeas

GLOSSARY OF FLOWERS

The flowers listed below are suitable for drying and most of the varieties are available commercially. The majority of the flowers are featured in this book but it is not a definitive list; it should be treated as a useful guide when choosing flowers for your displays.

Botanical name	Common name	Description
A		
Acacia dealbata	Mimosa/wattle	Fern-like leaves with tiny soft yellow bobble flowers
Acanthus mollis	Acanthus	Very tall stems with purple and white flowers
Achillea filipendulina	Achillea Coronation gold	Large flat-headed tall stems, yellow flowers
Achillea millefolium	Yarrow	White, pale pink to cerise with flat-headed blooms
Achillea ptarmica	The pearl	Soft white clusters of small flat-headed bobbly flowers
Achillea taygetea	Moonshine	Flat-headed pale sulphur-yellow flowers
Aconitum ranunculaceae	Monkshood	Tall deep blue/lilac flowers (poisonous)
Adenanthus cygnorum	Woolly bush	Grey/green spiky leaved shrub
Adenanthus cuneata	Retusa leaf	Spiky branches with rounded leaves along the stem, clustered towards tip
Adiantum cenustum	Maidenhair fern	Fronds on purple-black stalks, narrowly triangular. Deep olive green when dried
Agapanthus orientalis	African lily	Tallish stalks with spidery stick cluster to the tips
Agonis linearaifolia	Ti-tree rosa	Mass of white flowers on tall spiky stems. Smaller flowers than Ti-tree 'swampy' see 'Leptospermum'
Aira sp	Hair grass. Agrostis	Very fine silky grass, often dyed when dry
Alchemilla mollis	Lady's mantle	Star-shaped small flowers carried in loose clusters, yellow-green calyce instead of petals
Allium aflatunense	Ornamental onion	Tall with ball-shaped head and pinkish star-shaped flowers
Allium porrum	Leek head	Pale mauve ball-shaped head
Althea rosea	Hollyhock	Very tall with large funnel-shaped flowers. Wide range of colours
Alyssum sp	Alyssum	Blue flowers in clusters at top of stems
Amaranthus viridis	Love-lies-bleeding	Green spiky plumes or purple/red plumes, both pyramid shaped
Ambrociana viridis	Ambrociana	Almost lime green, soft ferny leaves quite thickly spread

Botanical name	Common name	Description
Ammobium alatum	Winged everlasting sand flower	Small white round stubby petals forming daisy shapes, yellow centres
Anaphalis nubigena	Anaphalis	Off-white clusters of flowers on grey/green stems
Anigozanthus pulcherrimus	Kangaroo paw – yellow	Soft yellow mini-banana-shaped flowers
Anigozanthus rufus	Kangaroo paw – red rufus	Deep wine-red mini-banana-shaped flowers
Anigozanthus sp	Kangaroo paw – black	Mini-banana-shaped flowers in yellow, tipped with black
Anethum graveolens	Dill	Tall green stems with white lacey flowers
Aphyllanthes	Glixia daisy	Minute daisy-shaped flowers on spindly stems
Artemesia	Mugwort	Green spiky stems, flowers cream when dry
Aruncus	Goatsbeard	White pointed plumes
Arundinaria sp	Bamboo	Light-green pointed leaves with thick cream-coloured woody stems
Avena sativa	Field oats	Light green, gold when mature
B		
Banksia ashbyi	Ashbyi	These are all native to Australia. They come in varying forms: large round, long nut or large protruding fat shapes. Some resemble flowers, others are more like seed heads or loofahs
Banksia attenuata	Attenuata	
Banksia baxteri	Baxteri	
Banksia burdetti	Burdetti	
Banksia candolleana	Candolleana	
Banksia coccinea	Coccinea	
Banksia grandis	Bull banksia leaves	
Banksia hookerana	Hookerana	
Banksia laricina	Laricina nuts	
Banksia menziesii	Menziesii	
Banksia prionotes	Prionotes	
Banksia prostrata	Prostrata leaves	
Banksia prostrata	Prostrata bud	
Banksia sceptrum	Sceptrum	
Banksia speciosa	Speciosa/brown bud	
Banksia victoria	Victoria	
Beaufortia decussata	Decussata leaf	Long leaf, rather like the spine of a fish in shape, dark green-brown in colour

Botanical name	Common name	Description	Botanical name	Common name	Description
Beaufortia sparsa	Red bottle brush	Red poker-like flowers, tall stems with green spiky leaves	*Chrysanthemum vulgare*	Tansy	Tall wild flower, with yellow flat heads, made up of small bobbles
Betula pendula	Silver birch	Silver-leaved tree, flowers deepen in colour to almost brown when dried	*Clematis tangurica*	Clematis (seed heads)	Silvery wispy seed heads, resembling beards
Brachychiton populnens	Brown pod	Smallish curved brown pods filled with deep yellow seeds	*Conospermum crassinervium*	Tassel smoke	All variations of soft grey/white bobbly feather-like flowers
Briza maxima	Quaking grass (large)	Small pearl-shaped buds of varying size	*Conospermum flexuosum*	Elk smoke	
Briza media	Quaking grass (medium)		*Conospermum incurvum*	Feather smoke	
Briza minima	Quaking grass (small)		*Conospermum stoechadis*	Common smoke	
Briza segromi	Briza segromi	Long fine quivering grass	*Cortaderia selloana*	Pampas grass	Very tall, white/cream soft, feather-like grass plumes
Bromus formus	Brome grass	Thick ear-headed green grass, wispy and fluffy and quite tall	*Craspedia globosa*	Craspedia/billy buttons	Yellow round balls on stiff stems
Bupleurum	Philica/white tip filler	Stiff brown stems with olive green spiky leaves and small white bobbles in clusters at top of stem	*Cynara scolymus*	Globe artichoke	Large-headed vegetable, deep green-brown with pointed segment leaves in layers
Buxifolium	Buxifolium	Small leaf branch with soft grey tips	*Cynara sp*	Pink cardoon	Tall exotica with stiff artichoke-like pink petals
Buxus sempervirens	Box	Small deep-green, round leaves on short stems, evergreen	**D**		
C			*Dahlia sp*	Pom-pom dahlia	Various colours, dries in a tight ball-shaped bud
Cacalia sp	Tassel flower	Small white groups of flowers. Average size	*Delphinium consolida*	Larkspur	Long purple, blue, pink, red or white flowers filling either side of tall stems
Calendula officinalis	Pot marigold	Orange-yellow, daisy-shaped flowers	*Delphinium elatum*	Delphinium	Similar to larkspur but much larger stems and bigger florets
Callistemon sp	Albany bottle brush	Deep wine-red poker-shaped flower tips tall with long wispy grass, foliage-like	*Dipsacus sp*	Teasle	Prickly round-headed seed turning brown at maturity
Cannomois virgata	Bell stalk	Stiff brown stalks with buds at intervals on stem	*Dryandra formosa*	Dryandra	Round orange segmented buds on long stems with grey/green stiff fern-shaped leaves
Capsella	Cress	Mass of tiny leaves forming green haze, bushy	*Dryandra obtusa*	Obtusa leaf	Spiral, spiky, twisting leaf
Carex	Sedge	Reed-type plant. Brown with brown bobbles on top of stem	*Dryandra polycephala*	Dryandra	Long stems with small yellow ochre buds and long spiky leaves shooting off from each bud
Carthamus tinctorius	Dyer's saffron	Orange flowers on tall green stems, flowers protruding from green, pointed leaf cluster	*Dryandra quercifolia*	Dryandra	Large Banksia-type buds with holly-shaped leaves
Celosia argentea cristata	Cockscomb	Deep red-crested flower measuring 3-5 ins across	*Dryopteris filix-mas*	Male fern	Can be deep or grass green ranging from 2-4 ft in height
Celosia argentea cristata minima	Cockscomb	Smaller red-crested flowers	*Dubium sp*	Dubium	Long exotic stems capped with soft grey bobbly heads
Centaurea cynus	Cornflower	Sprays of pink, blue and white flowers	*Dudinea sp*	Dudinea	Red, orange or yellow masses of flowers, flat and open like small leaves
Centaurea macrocephala	Centaurea thistle	Very tall yellow thistle-shaped flower heads	**E**		
Chrysanthemum sp	Chrysanthemum	Many colours. The heads are much smaller when dried	*Echinops bannaticus*	Globe thistle	Grey/blue globular prickly heads
Chrysanthemum parthenium	Matricaria	Small pale yellow flat-headed bobbles	*Echinops ritro*	Globe thistle	Smaller blue steel globular heads
Chrysanthemum solidaster	Solidaster	Mass of small yellow flowers in clusters	*Erica cinerea*	Bell heather	A mass of small bell-shaped commonly bright pink flowers. Can turn a deeper colour when dried

Botanical name	Common name	Description
Eryngium maritimum	Sea holly	Cone-shaped metallic blue flowers
Eryngium planum	Sea holly 'mountain'	Clusters of deep-blue prickly thistle-type heads
Eryngium sp	Eryngium	Large-headed sea holly, long wispy layers covering heads of steel blue
Eucalyptus calophylla	Gum nut	Small bell-shaped buds
Eucalyptus gunnii	Round leaf eucalyptus	Silver/blue/green round leaves
Eucalyptus lehmanni	Bushy yate	Medium sized nuts forming clusters in points
Eucalyptus kruseana	Eucalypus leaves	Deep glossy-green pointed leaves (sometimes sold bleached or dyed)
Eucalyptus pulverulenta	Spiral eucalyptus	Rounded leaves in deep bottle green with blue tint. Leaves grown in spirals up the stem
Eucalyptus pyriformis	Mallee pear	Small brown almost square nut shapes with central round protusion

F

Botanical name	Common name	Description
Fagus sylvatica	Beech leaves	Copper/green leaves and nuts
Festuca glauca	Festuca grass	Varying colours of pink when dried

G

Botanical name	Common name	Description
Gomphrena globosa	Globe amaranth	Small clover-shaped flowers forming ball-shaped heads in various colours
Gossypium herbaceum	Cotton plant	White fluffy cotton-wool-type clusters
Gypsophila elegans	Gypsophila	Tiny white bobbly clusters
Gypsophila paniculata	Baby's breath/ Bristol fairy	Tiny white flowers which dry into a haze of tight white bobbles
Gypsophila rugosa	Broom bloom, wild gypsophila	Coarse natural beige-coloured bobbles on firm stems

H

Botanical name	Common name	Description
Hakea cucullata	Cup leak hakea	Mass of crinkly rounded leaves
Hakea pandanicarpa	Corked hakea	Single cork-type nut split into four sections
Hakea petiolaris	Pointed hakea	Brown clusters of open nuts
Hedera helix	Ivy	Deep glossy green pointed leaves, poisonous
Helichrysum angustifolium	Curry plant	Tiny bobbly flowers smelling strongly of curry
Helichrysum bracteatum	Everlasting strawflower	Everlasting daisy, paper-like petals in wide variety of colours
Helichrysum scorpioides	Seacrest	A soft furry-stemmed white rambling plant with small white flowers
Helichrysum sesamoides	Everlasting daisy	White with yellow centre. Small heads with paper-like petals

Botanical name	Common name	Description
Helichrysum stoechas	Sanfordii	Yellow bobbly flower heads made up of tiny individual star-shaped flowers
Helichrysum vestium	Everlasting strawflower	White shiny petals on stiff, furry white stems
Helipterum acroclinium	Acroclinium daisy	Varying shades of pink and white daisies both with yellow centres
Helipterum argyropsis	Brown eyes	Everlasting African daisy with dark brown centres
Helipterum sp	Red bonnie	Deep pink daisy with characteristic black centre
Helipterum subulifolium	Sunray daisy	Bright-yellow daisy
Heracleum sphondylium	Hogweed	Tall fleshy stems with white lacy star-shaped flower
Hordeum sp	Black-eared barley	Black-tipped wisps on the husks
Hordeum vulgare	Six-rowed barley	Green slim barley with wispy, pointed husks
Humulus lupulus	Hops	Green bobbly cone-shaped flowers
Hydrangea macrophylla	Mop-headed hydrangea	Large-headed flower made up of small florets. Muted colours of pinks, lilacs, reds and blues
Hydrangea paniculata	Panicled hydrangea	Longer pointed flower heads with similar individual florets
Hypericum sp	St John's wort	This is poisonous, but very attractive with hard black berries and green foliage

I

Botanical name	Common name	Description
Immortellen sp	Ixodia achilleoides	South Australian daisy, small white flowers on hard wide fleshy stems

J

Botanical name	Common name	Description
Jacaranda mimosifolia	Jacaranda pod	Oval, brown split pods
Juncus sp	Rush	Long tubular grass with attractive hard, brown flowers

K

Botanical name	Common name	Description
Kingia australis	Djingarra leaf	Graceful flopping bell-shaped flowers in white/cream/brown on tubular stems

L

Botanical name	Common name	Description
Lagurus ovatus	Hair's tails	Stems terminate in fluffy, white/cream ovoid heads
Lavandula officinalis	Lavender	Grey/blue flowers borne in spikes, very pleasant aroma fresh and dried
Lepidium rurale	Lepidium	Mass of small leaves on bushy stems, a green haze of leaves
Leptospermum ellipticum	Ti-tree swampy	Little flowers the length of the stems, natural/white tiny coarse leaves
Leptospermum parviceps	Ti-tree coarse	Similar to above

Botanical name	Common name	Description
Leucodendron sp	Leucodendron	Branches of flat, rounded leaves with beige/pink flowers terminating at the tip of the stem, the same shape as the leaves
Leucodendron pubescens	Small cone leucodendron	Pink/brown cones with white fluff between the cone layers
Leucodendron rubrum	Plumosum/ tolbos top brush	Star-shaped cones on thick stems
Leucodendron teretifolium	Sabulosum	Light brown clusters of small brown cones
Leucodendron stelligenum	Leucodendron	Little brown cones within smooth flat leaves
Livistona speciosus	Palm spear	Stiff palm-shaped spear usually cream on tough stalk
Lysinema ciliata	Curry and rice	Attractive branches with long spiky flowers in beige, brown and cream
Limonium sinuatum	Statice	Many colours including mauve, pink, yellow, white, salmon and blue. Flat clusters of flowers papery petals on thick fleshy stems
Limonium tatarica latifolium	Sea lavender	White, heather-type plant, tiny white/pink flowers
Limonium latifolium	Sea lavender, caspia	Similar to above but longer wilder stems
Limonium suworowii	Pink poker	Long thin poker-shaped flowers in pinky mauve
Linum sp	Flax	Little yellow/beige bobbles on long thin stems
Lonos indorra	Lonas	Flat-headed yellow bobbled clusters, long stems
Lunaria rediviva	Honesty	Flat, round seed heads, brown outer husk, silver white lining
Lunaria rediviva sp	Mini honesty	Tiny green circles forming leaves
Brunia nodiflora	Silver brunia	Soft grey felt-like bobbles on tough strangely shaped stalks

M

Botanical name	Common name	Description
Milium sp	Millet	Tall grassy kernels of yellow gold on long stems
Molucella laevis	Bells of Ireland	Impressive stems with bell-shaped blooms turning from green to cream when dry

N

Botanical name	Common name	Description
Nelumbo lucifera	Lotus flower (pod)	Large flat-headed pod with series of evenly spaced holes where seeds have fallen
Nigells Damascena	Love-in-a-mist	Blue flowers and seed pods which are naturally green with deep red bars running down the pod

P

Botanical name	Common name	Description
Paeonia lactiflora	Peony	Large rose-shaped flowers of various colours. Often light pink and crimson
Papaver rhoeas	Field poppy	Small grey/brown seed pods remain when dried
Papaver somniferum	Opium poppy	Bulbous flat-capped grey seed heads
Papyrus gigantum	Papyrus	Tall wooden-type leaves
Passerina vulgaris	Vlei rose	Clusters of small pointed cones on stalks
Pennisetum sp	Pennisetum	Soft beige fluffy-headed grass type
Phaoenocoma prolifera	Phaoenocoma shrub	Vivid pink daisy-shaped flower heads crowded on the shrub
Phalaris aruninacea	Reed canary grass phalaris	Soft green clover-type grass heads
Phleum pratense	Timothy grass	Long soft narrow green heads
Phlomis fruticosa	Jerusalem sage	Ovate wedge-shaped leaves, whorls of yellow flowers appearing in the upper leaf axils
Physalis alkekengi franchetti	Chinese lanterns/ cape gooseberry	Orange lantern-shaped pods on rambling stems
Physocarpus sp	Physocarpus	Yellow beige lantern-shaped pods with central berry sometimes showing when pod splits
Physopsis spicata	Sago bush	White soft bobbly clusters resembling 'sago'
Pinus sp	Pine cone	Pine cone nut
Pithocarpa corymbulosa	Everlasting daisy	Miniature everlasting daisy, little white flowers on spindly stems
Pittosporum tenuifolium	Pittosporum	Small evergreen leaves deep green/brown when glycerined
Protea barbigera	Barbigera	Pink protea, extra large
Protea compacta	Compacta bud	Wooden-type flower with zigzag petals
Protea laurifolia	Laurifolia	Wooden-type flower with curling petals
Protea longifolia	Longifolia	Layered outer stiff petals of white and dark brown. White woolley interior
Protea nerifolia sp	Nerifolia	Various types, but generally soft shaving brush-type flower with curled exterior leaves
Protea nerifolia sp	Nerifolia	Soft cream plume-type leaves with dark interior
Protea macrophylla	Macrophylla	Light brown wooden-looking rosette with pointed petals
Protea grandiceps	Grandiceps	Long protea bud in red
Protea obtusifolia	Obtusifolia	Layered protea in red and yellow with long pointed petals

Botanical name	Common name	Description	Botanical name	Common name	Description
Protea recondita	Recondita	Curled wooden-looking bud in brown	**S**		
Protea repens sp	Repens	Pointed cream protea with red tips	*Salvia labiatae sp*	Salvia	Deep lilac, shaped in pointed stems not dissimilar to lavender
Protea repens sp	Repens	Huge wooden-looking flower	*Scirpus sp*	Club rush	Deep brown shiny grass with small tufts
Protea repens sp	Repens	Large protea cream with brown ribs	*Scabiosa atropurpurea*	Paper moon scabious	Papery seed heads
Protea repens sp	Repens	Medium cream with brown ribs	*Serruria sp*	Silky serruria	Soft, small cotton-wool-type buds in clusters
Protea suzanne	Rosette	Rounded rosette-type wooden-looking flower	*Setatia verticillata*	Polypogon grass	Soft green grass with fluffy tips
Pteronia paniculata	Cressia	Yellow ochre stubby flower, shoots on thickish stems	*Silene pendula*	Campion/ catch fly	Tiny, delicate pink flowers resembling little stars, rather fragile stems
Q			*Solidago compositae sp*	Golden rod	Long yellow/green stems with mass of very small flowers and leaves
Quercus fagacea	Oak	Jigsaw-puzzle-shaped leaves, dark brown when glycerined	*Stavia radiata*	Glass eyes	African heather-type daisies, very tiny heads growing in masses
Quercus robur	Oak (nuts)	Acorns	*Stipa pennata*	Feather grass	Silvery buff plumes
R			*Stirlingia latifolia*	Stirlingia	Little soft bobbles on black shiny stems
Rhododendron	Rhododendron	Pink, yellow, red and white, large open flowers with bell-shaped floppy petals	**T**		
Rosa Paleander	Rose	Pink	*Tilia vulgaris*	Lime	Mid-green rounded leaves, but pointed in shape on thin brown stalks
Rosa Paleander 'joy'	Rose	Dark purple	*Tetraria speciosissima*	Weeping grass	Long, flexible deep-brown grasses with stubby tufts growing up the stems
Rosa Paleander	Rose	Lilac	*Triticum aestirum*	Field wheat	Grass with stubbly-eared tops, light green to gold when ripe
Rosa Paleander	Rose	Red	**V**		
Rosa Golden times	Rose	Yellow	*Verticordia brownii*	Cauliflower plant	A finer version of the vegetable. Masses of soft yellow florets forming a flat-topped head; often dyed
Rosa Paleander 'Selina'	Rose	Dark red			
Rosa 'Gerda'	Rose	Pink			
Rosa Europe	Rose	Lilac			
Rosa Sonia	Rose	Pink	*Verticordia densiflora*	Densiflora	Little pink/lilac bobble flowers on spindly brown stalks
Rosa Lamenuette	Rose	Apricot			
Rosa Polka	Rose	Light lilac	*Verticordia nitens*	Golden morrison	Soft, orange, flat clusters on long stiff stalks
Rosa Veronica	Rose	Light pink	**X**		
Rosa Zurella	Rose	Dark lilac	*Xeranthemum abbum*	Everlasting xeranthemum	Lilac or cream daisy-type flowers on silver stems
Rosa Sweet Sonia	Rose	Light pink			
Rosa Ilona	Rose	Dark red	*Xylomelum augustifolium*	Woody pear	Soft grey pears on rigid brown stalks, little pointed leaves
Rosa Pink ilsetta	Rose	Pink			
Rosa Jaguar	Rose	Dark red	**Z**		
Rosa Mercedes	Rose	Red	*Zea mays*	Sweet corn	Long orange, yellow or gold corn husks 6-8 in long
Rosa Anja	Rose	Pink			
Rosa Jack frost	Rose	Cream	*Zinnia elegans*	Zinnia	Similar to dahlia when dried, ball-shaped mass of petals
Rosa Belinda	Rose	Dark orange			

These rose varieties are now available commercially

Botanical name	Common name	Description
Ruscus sp	Butcher's broom	Short busy stems with a mass of sharp pointed deep-green small leaves, evergreen

ACKNOWLEDGEMENTS

My special thanks to photographer, Simon McBride, for his invaluable help and commitment to the book. My thanks also to Alyson Gregory for her unlimited time and help with the editing; and to Vic Giolitto for his imaginative design. I also want to thank friends who lent their homes for the location work: Jennifer and David Curling; Patricia and Nick Woodifield; John Clark; Eliza and Martin Lamb; John and Fiona St Cyres; Antony and Susan Wood; Roger Chubb; Jay Ruperelia; Christiane. Particular thanks to Justin and Michelle Cadbury whose beautiful home and generous hospitality contributed to some wonderful photographs. Thanks to the Overhills for lending the cart; Nick and Janie Herrtage for their hospitality; Alan and Sara Paston Williams; Stewart and Carolyn Westaway. Thanks to Ruth Hayes-Davis, Miriam Fishwick, Cheryl Brown, Christine Berry and Katey Biebly at Hay Fever. Finally thanks to my mother and brother for their support and to my children Jessica and Jason who saw so little of me while I was writing this book.

I would also like to thank Daan and Tromp Hogewoning, my Dutch flower suppliers, for being wonderful hosts; Rochelle and Rosemary of R&R Flowers; Mike Braham of Savannah Marketing; Dina Wulfsohn, of Wulfsohn and James; NEXT Interiors, Staks and to Gidleigh Park Hotel, Chagford, Devon, for permission to take photographs in the reception rooms (pages 61, 68, 75, 108, 109).

LIST OF SUPPLIERS

Hay Fever Dried Flowers, 4 Cathedral Close, EXETER, Devon EX1 1EZ, retailers of dried flowers, and basketware.

Flowers, Basketware and Containers were supplied by the following:

Addresses

NEXT Interiors,
54–60 Kensington
High Street
London W8 4NJ

Nationwide retail vases, fabrics and dried flowers

R & R Flowers
35 Muswell Road
London N10 2BS
England

Wholesale African Flowers

Wulfsohn & James Ltd,
12 Campden Grove
London W8 4JG
England

Wholesale Australian flowers and basketware

Savannah Marketing
106 Claverham Road
Yatton,
Bristol BS19 4LE
England

Wholesale African flowers

A & S Designs Ltd
174 Estcourt Road
London SW6 7HD
England

Wholesale basketware

Machin and Henry International
Unit 103, Building A
Faircharm Trading Estate
Creekside,
London SE8 3DX
England

Whole flowers and basketware

Staks
Harlequin Centre
Exeter
Devon
England

Vases nationwide retail

159

INDEX